Dauntless Women

illustrations by

RAFAEL PALACIOS

Dauntless Women

STORIES OF PIONEER WIVES

by *Winifred Mathews*

Biography Index Reprint Series

 BOOKS FOR LIBRARIES PRESS
FREEPORT, NEW YORK

INTERNATIONAL STANDARD BOOK NUMBER:

0-8369-8031-X

LIBRARY OF CONGRESS CATALOG CARD NUMBER:

70-126325

PRINTED IN THE UNITED STATES OF AMERICA

Dedicated to

ALL THOSE WHO ARE EAGER TO RESPOND TO THE
CHALLENGE OF CHRISTIAN PIONEER WORK IN THEIR
OWN DAY WITH THE COURAGE AND DEVOTION OF
THESE PIONEER WOMEN OF AN EARLIER GENERATION

Contents

ACKNOWLEDGMENTS

Grateful acknowledgment is made to the following:

ANN JUDSON—*Dr. Adoniram Judson: Memoir of the Life and Labours,* by Francis Wayland, 2 vols. (London, J. Nisbet, 1853); *Adoniram Judson,* by Edward Adoniram Judson (Philadelphia, American Baptist Publication Society, 1894); *Ann of Ava,* by Ethel Daniels Hubbard (New York, Missionary Education Movement, 1941).

MARY MOFFAT—*Lives of Robert and Mary Moffat,* by John Smith Moffat (New York, A. C. Armstrong & Son, 1888); *Missionary Labours and Scenes in South Africa,* by R. Moffat (London, John Snow, 1842).

MARY LIVINGSTONE—*Missionary Travels and Researches in South Africa,* by David Livingstone (London, John Murray, 1857); *The Personal Life of David Livingstone,* by W. G. Blaikie (London, John Murray, 1880); *Livingstone,* by R. J. Campbell (London, Ernest Benn, 1929).

CHRISTINA COILLARD—*Coillard of the Zambesi,* by C. W. Mackintosh (London, Ernest Benn, 1907); *François Coillard: A Wayfaring Man,* by Edward Shillito (New York, George H. Doran, 1923).

MARY WILLIAMS—*Memoirs of the Life of the Rev. John Williams,* by Ebenezer Prout (New York, Robert Carter, 1850); *A Narrative of Missionary Enterprises in the South Sea Islands,* by John Williams (London, John Snow, 1840).

AGNES WATT—*Agnes C. P. Watt: Twenty-five Years' Mission Life on Tanna, New Hebrides* (1896).

LILLIAS UNDERWOOD—*Fifteen Years among the Top-Knots or Life in Korea,* by L. H. Underwood (New York, American Tract Society, 1904); *Underwood of Korea,* by Lillias H. Underwood (New York, Fleming H. Revell, 1918); *The Call of Korea,* by H. G. Underwod (New York, Fleming H. Revell, 1908).

Steel-true and blade-straight
The great artificer
Made my mate . . .
Teacher, tender, comrade, wife,
A fellow-farer true through life.

—*Robert Louis Stevenson*

PROLOGUE

*I*n Christian heroism she proved the equal of her intrepid husband, and in patient endurance his superior." Thus wrote the biographer of John Williams about Mary, the wife of that Christian pioneer and martyr of the South Seas. A reading of that biography and of many similar stories of Christian heroism created a desire in the writer to rescue Mary Williams and other missionary wives from the musty volumes in which their stories lie embalmed and to present them as women of flesh and blood who actually lived and suffered and triumphed in the past century.

In many Oriental lands, in many parts of Africa, in the islands of the Pacific, the wife of a missionary was the first white woman ever seen by the native peoples. We cannot easily exaggerate the importance of this fact or the influence that these Christian white women exerted over primitive peoples among whom women were at best the burden-bearers whose lot was to work and obey, and who were often treated with active or passive cruelty. The Christian homes, where God was confessed in "the beauty of their ordered lives," would have been impossible if these rare women had been unwilling to leave all and follow him. Perhaps no form of witness is more fruitful than that of the Christian home in the non-Christian world as a center of sacrificial service to the community around.

The heartache and the joy of planting these homes in the wilderness are seen in the stories of Christina Coillard, whose home for years was a traveling wagon in South Africa; of Agnes Watt on a South Sea island, who had to put every movable object hurriedly away whenever her "savage" friends came to call; of Mary Moffat at Kuruman, who for over forty years mothered all who needed her care without distinction of race, nation, color, or religion; and of many others. The white traders of that time who went to the remote corners of the world without their wives and families more often than not entered into relationships with the native women that made the Christian home life of the missionaries shine more brightly by contrast.

The day of the unmarried woman missionary, whose service is now so valuable, had not yet arrived. No woman could go to the mission field save as a wife. A hundred years ago zenana work, teaching in mission schools, and medical missions to women had hardly been thought of. And many a woman who ardently desired to serve God in some remote part of his world was grateful for the opportunity of marriage to a missionary who, on his side, had been advised by his mission board to marry before he was sent to some lonely outpost. We must not assume that romance never entered into these unions, or that they were any less happy because the wife was often attracted to the missionary before she married the man.

Each of these missionary wives would be the first to ask to be portrayed not as a saint but as a faulty human being:

> *A creature not too bright or good*
> *For human nature's daily food.*

Yet without them their respective husbands would have been like birds trying to fly with one wing. If they had not worked among the women while their husbands taught the men, the churches established as a result of the men's work would have lacked depth and permanence.

The activities of husband and wife were so closely intertwined that in most cases the story of the wife has had to be built up from a biography written primarily about the husband. Thousands of pages have been scanned for the precious sentences in diaries or letters that reveal the woman's point of view or special contribution. Every incident and every conversation has its basis in an authentic record, and the conversations reproduce in direct speech the language in which these men and women of another generation expressed their thoughts and sentiments in letters and diaries.

Ann Judson

Two ladies in rustling silk gowns were enjoying a sedate gossip one bitter winter afternoon of the year 1812 in the New England seaport town of Salem, Massachusetts.

"I hear that Miss Hasseltine is going to India!" said one. "Why does she go?"

"Why, she thinks it her duty. Wouldn't you go if you thought it your duty?"

"I," replied her friend tartly, "would not think it my duty."

Ann Hasseltine, called Nancy by friends, whose beauty and intelligence had been the talk of her native town of Bradford, Massachusetts, was now being talked about for a different reason. It was "preposterous," "wild," "improper," for her to be ready to do what no American woman before her had ever done. But Nancy herself was full of quiet determination. Writing to a friend in the somewhat formal style of the period, she told her that "my determinations are not hasty or formed without viewing the dangers, trials and hardships attendant on a missionary life. Nor were my determinations formed in consequence of an attachment to any earthly object; but with a sense of my obligation to God, with a full conviction of its being a call of providence, and consequently my duty."

The call of duty had come to her in the form of a proposal of marriage from the handsome, forceful young minister, Adoniram Judson, who, with three college friends, had besought the Congregational churches of Massachusetts to form a missionary society and send them as the first Christian emissaries from North America to the Orient. Without presuming to doubt Nancy's own statement that her determination to accept God's call to missionary work was not formed "in consequence of an attachment to any earthly object," we may at least believe that she found it easier to take the path of duty because she would walk in it with a beloved companion. Adoniram, imaginative and sensitive, responsive to beauty and dependent on affection, had been instantly attracted by the gay, lovely, popular girl, in whom he discerned a deep love for their Master and a desire to serve him. She refused his offer of marriage at first because of a natural fear of the unknown life to which she would commit herself, but the appeal in Adoniram's remarkably brilliant hazel eyes was a very effective reinforcement of the promptings of conscience.

When Nancy Hasseltine became Mrs. Adoniram Judson one snowy day in February, 1812, she was twenty-three, her husband a year older. Strong in their love for God and for each other, they faced the dim, uncertain future with high hope and courage when they set sail for India a few days later.

During the four months' voyage, Adoniram studied books about the Baptist theological position in preparation for their expected meetings in India with the great English Baptist missionary, William Carey. In a letter home Ann wrote: "I frequently told him, if he became a Baptist *I would not.*" But later she had to confess, "We are now confirmed Baptists, not because we wished to be, but because truth compelled us to be. . . . We feel that we are alone in the world, with no real friend but each other, no one on whom we can depend but God." William Carey baptized Adoniram and Ann on September 6, 1812, in the Baptist chapel in Calcutta.

The plight of the two young people who had thus cut themselves off from any financial support (for the Baptists in America had no foreign mission board and they were dependent on loans from the English Baptists in India) was aggravated by the war that existed between the United States and Britain, and by the refusal of the British East India Company to allow missionaries of any nationality to work in the territory that it controlled. William Carey and his associates were established at Serampore, in the small portion of India that remained in Danish hands.

For more than a year after Ann and her husband landed at Calcutta in June, 1812, they were seeking a place where they would be allowed to work in peace. Pursued by warrants for their arrest, by orders that they should be sent back immediately to America and then that they should go to England, they fled by one ship after another from port to port as if they had been criminals. They were invited to settle on Mauritius, but their hearts were set on an unopened field. Finally they had to make an immediate choice—either to take the first boat to sail from Madras, whatever its destination, or be bundled off ignominiously to Britain. Even their fortitude wavered when they learned that the destination of the only ship by which they could escape was Rangoon, the port of Burma, a country that was at that time in the grip of one of the most cruel and horrifying despotisms the world has ever known. Ann's journal reflects the struggle: "Adieu to polished, refined Christian society. Our lot is not cast among you, but among pagans, among barbarians, whose tender mercies are cruel. Indeed, we voluntarily forsake you and for Jesus' sake choose the latter for our associates."

The three weeks' voyage from Madras to Rangoon, in an old and unseaworthy vessel, was a nightmare. Their only cabin was a shelter of canvas rigged up on deck, buffeted by high winds on the stormy voyage and often awash with water. Ann was so ill that she had to be carried ashore at Rangoon, where they landed on July 14, 1813. She saw "a miserable, dirty town, the houses being built with bamboo and teak planks, with thatched roofs, almost without drainage, and intersected by muddy creeks through which the tide flowed at high water."

In all the land of Burma only one Protestant Christian missionary was working, and he had made not a single convert. He was Felix, William Carey's eldest son, who had married a Burmese woman and lived with her in native style. His missionary work, however, was subordinated to service in the court of the king of Burma, and eventually he gave up the mission altogether. Four Roman Catholic priests were in the country; but since one of their secret Burmese converts, betrayed to the government by his nephew, had been tortured and beaten almost to death by the dreaded iron mall, they had not attempted to spread their faith, and ministered solely to the descendants of foreign settlers in Burma.

Some six months after her arrival, Ann was taken by a French lady to visit the wife of the viceroy. While waiting, they were entertained by the secondary wives, who examined the two white women with insatiable curiosity. But fastidious Ann felt disconcerted when the none-too-clean Burmese women calmly tried on her bonnet, gloves, and shawl, although she managed to conceal her feelings. When the vicereine came in, richly dressed and smoking a long silver pipe, the inferior wives retired to a respectful distance. She spoke very graciously to Ann, but showed as much unbridled curiosity as the other wives. Was Ann her husband's first wife? How many other wives had he? How many children had she?

Then the viceroy himself came in, and Ann told Adoniram afterwards that she really trembled when she looked at this high official, for never before had she seen such a savage-looking creature. He carried an enormous spear, and with a nod of his head could condemn anyone he pleased to instant execution without trial.

The vicereine took a great fancy to the eager and charming young woman in her best high-waisted muslin dress and the demure bonnet that failed to hide her irrepressible dark brown curls. She asked Ann to visit her every day, and in the months to come treated her with marked affection. Occasionally she permitted Ann to talk to her about Jesus Christ, and accepted a copy of Adoniram's translation into Burmese of the Gospel of St. Matthew. She even commanded one of her daughters to memorize a catechism written by Ann. It seemed to Ann, however, that the vicereine was actuated more by a desire to be pleasant than by any real interest in Christianity.

It is surprising that after only six months in the country Ann should know the very difficult Burmese language sufficiently well to be able to talk with the vicereine, particularly as she and Adoniram had to learn it from a teacher who could not speak a word of English, and without the aid of a grammar or dictionary. Ann had an advantage over her husband because in her management of the household she had to pick up some Burmese words at once or they would have starved. At the end of a year she found that "I can talk and understand others better than Mr. Judson, though he knows really much more about the nature and construction of the language than I do." From seven o'clock in the morning till ten o'clock at night Adoniram sat with his Burmese teacher. Ann, too, studied the language, although at first the teacher felt it beneath his dignity to waste his skill on a mere woman!

Life was not easy "with no dear Christian friends" in a country that Ann describes as "in a most deplorable state, full of darkness, idolatry and cruelty, full of commotion and uncertainty," governed by capricious officials who extorted bribes from those in their power and who in turn bribed those above them, in an unbroken chain leading up to the king himself. The fierce heat of Rangoon, heavy with moisture, was debilitating, and there were none of the modern aids that now make life bearable in such a climate. Fevers of all kinds were an ever present menace. "But," writes the young wife in the letter in which she gives this gloomy picture, and we can imagine the glow in her face as she does so, "we are still happy in each other. . . . We both unite in saying that we never were happier, never more contented in any situation than the present. We feel that this is the post to which God has appointed us."

Ann had no illusions about "the native innocence and purity of heathen nations. . . . Let those who hold such beliefs," she writes, "visit Burma! The system of religion here [Buddhism] has no power over the heart or restraint on the passions. It is like an alabaster image, perfect and beautiful in all its parts, but destitute of life. . . . It provides no atonement for sin. Here also the gospel triumphs over this and every other religion in the world."

Against this dark background of life in Rangoon, a few joys stood out in piercing relief. Imagine, if you can, the day on which Ann received the first mail from home since leaving family and friends in America two and a half years earlier. Imagine, too, the prayers of thankfulness from two lonely hearts when she and Adoniram learned that the Baptists of America had formed a foreign missionary society to support them and recruit other workers.

The birth of their first child, Roger Williams, in September, 1815, with Adoniram as sole attendant, brought exquisite happiness to both parents. But it was short-lived; within eight months the baby developed symptoms of fever, and in spite of the simple remedies prescribed by a Portuguese Roman Catholic priest, died after a short illness. Ann's letter to a friend in America at this time is a cry echoed from the hearts of many pioneer women: "If you have never lost a first-born, an only son, you cannot *know* my pain. Had you even buried your little boy, you are in a Christian country, surrounded by friends and relatives who could soothe your anguish and direct your attention to other objects. But behold us, solitary and alone, with this one single source of recreation! Yet even this must be removed, to show us that we need no other source of enjoyment but God Himself!" Faith triumphs in this dark hour, and she adds: "Do not think, though I thus write, that I repine at the dealings of Providence, or would wish them to be otherwise than they are. No; 'though He slay me, yet will I trust in Him' is the language I would adopt."

Within a few months Ann experienced the almost overpowering joy of companionship with a like-minded woman, Mrs. Hough, the wife of the first missionary sent to help Judson in the mission. To talk to another woman in English, after years during which she had been denied that simple blessing, was like the first draught of cool water to a man dying of thirst in the desert. About the same time a printing press and set of Burmese type arrived as a gift from the English Baptists in Serampore, and Mr. Hough set to work at once, single-handed, to print a Burmese grammar and tract that Adoniram had already prepared.

During their first five years in Rangoon the Judsons did not make a single convert, although a few inquirers braved probable persecution to discuss Christianity with them. On all hands they were told that it would ruin a Burman to adopt the new religion, and the inquirers made their visits to Judson secretly, lapsing into silence and leaving as soon as another visitor made his appearance. Every Sunday some twenty or thirty Burmese women, however, gathered to talk with Ann about the God who, to their inexpressible astonishment, loved women equally with men.

The viceroy and his friendly wife were recalled to Ava in 1818, and in Adoniram's absence on a voyage to Chittagong, officials of the new viceroy summoned Mr. Hough to a succession of ignominious and irritating examinations lasting for hours at a time, during which he was warned that "if he did not tell the truth relative to his situation in the country, they would write it with his heart's blood." The new viceroy scarcely knew the Judsons, and as he had left his family behind in Ava, Ann could not ask his wife to intercede on behalf of Mr. Hough, who did not know from day to day what fate was in store for him. In this extremity Ann had the courage to ignore Burmese etiquette, which decreed that no woman should appear at court in the absence of the vicereine, and approached the viceroy as he sat in state, surrounded by officers. On hearing her petition, he sternly rebuked the officers who were responsible for ill-treating Mr. Hough and commanded them to cease molesting him in any way. The officers, of course, were hoping that the missionaries would buy Mr. Hough's freedom with bribes, and did not dream that their malicious purpose would be defeated by the daring action of this gentle foreign woman.

The danger passed, but its consequences remained: a large number of the women in Ann's class and of the other inquirers ceased to visit the missionaries as soon as it was known that they had come under unfavorable notice from government officials. A terrible epidemic of cholera that swept the city for the first time in its history frightened the people still further.

Meanwhile the Houghs left Rangoon for Calcutta, but were replaced in time by two other missionaries and their wives. Alas, one young couple soon had to leave on account of the husband's health, and he died at sea on the way to India.

One Sunday in June, 1819, Adoniram and Ann, the Colmans, and a few Burmese inquirers gathered at the edge of a large pond near the wayside preaching house where Judson had begun public preaching a few months before. In a spirit of solemn and searching consecration Judson baptized the first

Burmese convert, who had lived for some months in the benign Christian atmosphere of the mission house. The missionaries had solemnly warned this man that he had nothing to expect in this world but persecution, and perhaps death. Ann wrote that "this event, this trophy of victorious grace has filled our hearts with sensations hardly to be conceived by Christians living in Christian countries. It seems to encourage us to hope that the Lord has other chosen ones in this place." The fear of persecution was so real that the next two converts begged to be baptized in the evening and in solitude. Judson agreed, on their assurance that "if actually brought before Government they could not think of denying their Saviour." Six years in Burma, three converts, and their work practically at a standstill!

One or two inquirers, who continued to visit the Judsons in secret, whispered that it was dangerous for them to stay in Rangoon and preach to the common people. "Go to Ava," they urged, "to see 'the lord of life and death.' If the king is brought to approve, the religion will spread rapidly; but no one will come to discuss religion with you now because they fear 'the owner of the sword.'" Ominous names for a king! But they had been more than earned by the cruel and despotic tyrants who had sat on the throne of Burma.

In December, 1819, therefore, Judson and Colman left Rangoon "to go up to the golden feet and lift our eyes to the golden face," in the flowery language of the pass to visit Ava that they obtained from the viceroy. It was a severe test of their faith to leave their wives alone in Rangoon, but unless they could get some assurance from the king that they were free to make converts, they felt they could scarcely continue their work. Two months later, after seven hundred miles of river travel by Burmese rowing-boat, they were back in Rangoon, utterly disheartened. Their offering, the English Bible printed in six volumes, each volume bound in gold-leaf and enclosed in a rich embroidered cover, had been refused, they themselves had been abused, and all that they had learned of the fierce new king added to their apprehensions. The Judsons' letters at this time are full of torturing doubts. Should they trust in God and continue the mission although prohibited by the government and exposed to persecution? But "can we bear to see our dear disciples in prison, in fetters, under torture? Can we stand by them and encourage them to bear patiently the rage of their persecutors? Are we willing to participate with them? Though the spirit may be sometimes almost willing, is not the flesh too weak?"

Their fears were rebuked when the three converts entreated the missionaries not to leave them, and declared that they would suffer persecution, even death, rather than renounce Christ. "Stay at least," they urged, "until a little church of ten is collected and a native teacher is set over it, and then if you must go we will not say nay. In that case the religion will spread of itself. The emperor cannot stop it."

In the face of this conviction, what could the Judsons do but stay? The Colmans went to Chittagong, outside Burmese jurisdiction, to start another mission there; and Adoniram and Ann, with their three converts, remained alone in Rangoon to continue their witness. To their overwhelming joy, seven more Burmans were baptized during the next five months. They included the first woman, Mah-men-la. She, with other women, had spent whole days with Ann, while her husband and his friends were talking with Adoniram. Mah-men-la, Ann's first Burmese Christian sister, was at that time "fifty-one years old, of most extensive acquaintance through the place, of much strength of mind, decision of character and consequent influence over others." Entirely on her own initiative, she opened a village school; until that time the only school was one conducted by Buddhist priests.

Ann was teaching and praying with these Burmese women, and trying to bring them to the point of decision while she herself was so ill with a serious liver complaint that she was unable to leave the couch or walk across the room without violent suffering. With her yellow, emaciated face, her hair lank and lusterless, she bore little resemblance to the blooming young girl who had been the belle of Bradford, Massachusetts. In July, 1819, Adoniram had accompanied her on the long journey to Calcutta, where she received medical treatment and temporary relief. But two years later she had to leave him alone in Rangoon while she returned to America. Adoniram was almost certain that his beloved Ann, the one faithful companion of the years of disappointment and dawning hope, would not survive the long voyage, although it offered the only possibility of returning health. Ann, weakened by long suffering and racked by continual anxiety for her husband in his solitary and dangerous situation, was tempted to turn back even while she was waiting in Calcutta for a ship.

October, when Ann returned to her parents' home, is the most beautiful month of the year in New England. The flaming glory of maple and sumac fired the hills and woods. Ann gazed out of the window of the stage coach on the last lap of her long journey and drank in refreshing draughts of the tangy autumn breeze, so exhilarating after the moist and stagnant air of Rangoon. In the wan face of the woman who had left them seven years earlier as a radiant girl, her parents and sisters saw indelible marks of suffering and endurance, but also of a spiritual beauty and serenity that more than compensated for the loss of youthful bloom. For six exciting weeks relatives, friends, and neighbors crowded into the hospitable Hasseltine home to see and hear this young woman who had had experiences never even dreamed of by the sedate, stay-at-home New Englanders. Ann made real to them the far-off people of Burma with all their fears and spiritual poverty. She was most happy when she was telling them about the Burmese converts and inquirers and all the apprehensions and hopes for the future that she shared with her husband. Soon, however, she became alarmingly ill, and went south for treatment. From months in a sick room she emerged stronger in health, with the manuscript of a book on the history of the American mission in Burma, and with a faith that had gained fresh radiance and resilience.

Before sailing for Burma in June, 1823, she paid a fleeting visit home, full of the great news, which had come to her in a letter from Adoniram, that he had baptized three more of the Burmese women whom she had taught, and for whom she prayed constantly and intensely. Many people in America remembered her "profound religious feeling" and pronounced her "one of the most fascinating of women."

So thought Adoniram that December day in 1823 when she landed in Rangoon after an absence of two years and four months. To the weary, lonely man the return of this loving companion in renewed health and beauty brought fresh life and courage. Eagerly he claimed her sympathy for their next move. An astounding transformation seemed to have come about in the Burmese king's attitude. Dr. Price, a newly arrived medical missionary from America, was performing operations, and his praises reached the royal court at Ava. When Price was summoned by the king, he was accompanied by Adoniram as interpreter, and both missionaries were graciously received. The king invited Judson to return to live permanently in "the golden city" of Ava.

Leaving the growing work in Rangoon in charge of the Houghs, who had returned from Calcutta, the reunited husband and wife set out on the long, idyllic river journey. The boat's pace was so slow that often they walked for a while along the river banks and through the villages.

Having lived in Burma for several years, they were not surprised to find, when they arrived in Ava, that the capricious despot who occupied the throne was no longer interested in them and their mission, and that all the king's counselors and officials with whom Adoniram had made friends on his previous visit had been dismissed. Those who had taken their place naturally followed the king's lead in ignoring the missionaries. Notwithstanding this blow to their hopes, the Judsons went quietly on with their work. Ann opened a school for girls. The first two pupils, whom she adopted, she called Mary and Abby Hasseltine after her sisters.

Within a few months of their arrival in Ava, war broke out between Britain and Burma, and Rangoon was captured by the British Army in retaliation for audacious raids by the Burmans into British territory. One June day, in 1824, as Ann and Adoniram were at dinner, the door was rudely flung open and a prison official seized Judson on arrest as a spy of the British. He was dragged off, bound so tightly with a small, hard cord used by the Burmans as an instrument of torture that he could scarcely breathe. Before that terrible day was over, Ann heard from Moung Ing, one of the Christians from Rangoon who had accompanied them to Ava, that her husband and Dr. Price, together with three Englishmen, had been flung into the one dark, filthy room that comprised the "Hand-shrink-not" prison of death, already crowded with condemned criminals. Each was tethered with three pairs of iron fetters and fastened to a long pole in such a way that he was in excruciating pain. The city governor called to examine Ann and her possessions. He left guards to confine her and her Burmese servants to the house, so that to her crushing anxiety about her husband was added the final agony of her inability to help him. Shivering with apprehension lest she be found out, she managed to hide away a considerable sum of money before the house was searched.

Remembering the prevailing Burmese custom of bribery, Ann contrived to send a message to the governor asking to be allowed to bring him a present. He received her and her "present" graciously, gave her a passport into the prison, and introduced her to his head officer, an evil-looking man, who immediately demanded the equivalent of a hundred dollars as reward for a doubtful promise to make the prisoners more comfortable. Ann hurried to the prison. If she had known then on how many other occasions she was to see her husband crawl over the filthy floor to the entrance, his heavy fetters clanking, his unwashed, unshaven face ever more haggard, even her high courage, sustained by unwavering faith in God, might have faltered. Adoniram's face brightened with almost incredulous joy when he saw her, for during the two days since his arrest he had been tortured by fears of what was happening to her, alone and unprotected in the power of unscrupulous enemies. On her next visit to the prison she carried a pillow, so hard and uncomfortable that even the avarice of a Burmese jailer would not covet it. Into it she had sewn Adoniram's manuscript translation of the New Testament. It was the only copy, and if it were confiscated by the Burmans, the concentrated toil of years would be lost.

During the next eighteen months Ann's whole being was devoted to the threefold task of providing for the Burmese children and servants now wholly dependent on her, of getting food and clothing to her husband, to Dr. Price, and to the British prisoners, who otherwise would starve, and, most important of all, of securing their release from captivity.

In the hope of pleasing the highly nationalistic Burmans, Ann always wore one of the rich-colored silk Burmese skirts and muslin jackets given to her by the governor's wife, who became her staunch friend. With her dark curls brushed smoothly back from her brow and knotted on the top of her head in Burmese style, the beauty of her tall, slender figure enhanced by the long, tight skirt, she haunted the homes of members of the royal family and government officials, pleading the cause of the foreign prisoners. One of these officials kept her waiting from dawn until noon for an audience, and then dismissed her petition with contempt. As she turned away, he ordered her to give him her silk umbrella. Pleading the danger of sunstroke if she walked unprotected from the midday heat, she begged him for a paper parasol in exchange. With a laugh that mocked the agony that had reduced her from a robust woman to a shadow, he remarked that only stout people were in danger of sunstroke.

Daily she watched the prisoners grow thinner and more feeble, and endured the petty persecution and insults of the jailers. They often kept her waiting for hours before she saw her husband for a few moments, and demanded bribes before they would hand over the food and comforts that she carried to the captives.

Her courage, wit, and charm won her many friends who helped her secretly with gifts of food for the prisoners, and tried to create the impression in court circles that Judson and Price, as Americans, were not in any way responsible for the Anglo-Burmese war. None of these friends, however, dared to brave the anger of the royal tyrant by directly petitioning for the prisoners' release, especially as the Burmese armies were suffering one defeat after another at the hands of British troops. The city governor formed the habit of expecting Ann to visit him every other day to talk about Burmese customs, and even allowed her to erect a bamboo shelter in the prison yard where her husband was able from time to time to spend a few precious hours away from the sickening sights, sounds, and stench of the overcrowded prison.

Early in 1825, Ann's visits to the prison ceased, and Adoniram endured three weeks of cruel anxiety before she returned to the prison, having walked the two miles from the mission house with their second child in her arms. To this frail, blue-eyed baby, Maria, Adoniram wrote several stanzas, addressed "To an infant daughter, twenty days old, in the condemned prison at Ava."

On one of her daily visits to the prison, when Maria was about three months old, Ann found to her horror that Judson's bamboo shelter had been torn down and his precious pillow had disappeared. Adoniram and the other white prisoners had been spirited away. She hastened to the governor. In reply to her distracted entreaties for news, he told her, "You can do nothing more for your husband," adding with solemn emphasis, "Take care of yourself."

Disregarding his warning about her own safety, Ann threaded her way through the city streets, seeking for some trace of the missing men. A bystander said that they had been taken in the direction of Amarapura. Acting on this slender information, Ann at once bundled Mary and Abby Hasseltine, a devoted Bengali servant, baby Maria, and herself into a covered boat on the river. Two miles from Amarapura they had to take to a springless oxcart, which jolted violently on its solid wooden wheels along the hot, dusty highway. At the village Ann learned that the prisoners had passed through on their way to the Oung-pen-la prison. On they went under the scorching afternoon sun, reaching the new prison in the early evening. The prisoners, chained two and two, were huddled together on the ground. After a terrible forced march of many miles under the burning tropical sun, without head covering or shoes, Adoniram was almost too weak to notice his wife's presence. He did not tell her that all the prisoners believed that they were to be burned alive in the dilapidated building, as they had been told when they left Ava. This haunting fear was dispelled when a gang of workmen began to repair the prison. The general who had intended to enjoy the gruesome spectacle had himself been disgraced and executed.

Ann besought the jailer to find some place where she and the children could spend the night. He offered her one of the two rooms in his own house, filthy and half filled with grain, but Ann was thankful to call it home, not for one night only, but for several months. "All the money I could command in the world," she wrote afterwards, "I had brought with me, secreted about my person. But our Heavenly Father was better to us than our fears; for notwithstanding the constant extortions of the jailers during the whole six months we were at

Oung-pen-la, and the frequent straits to which we were brought, we never really suffered for the want of money, though frequently from the want of provisions, which were not procurable."

She nursed the children through an attack of smallpox and tended Adoniram, who was suffering from fever and exhaustion and the pain of his tormented feet. Under her loving care all her patients began to improve, but she herself fell victim to one of those virulent tropical diseases that in those days were almost always fatal to foreigners. For two months she lay in utter helplessness on a mat in a filthy, overcrowded hovel. Both she and Adoniram must have died but for the faithful and affectionate care of the Bengali cook, who "seemed to forget his caste, and almost his own wants in his efforts to serve us. . . . He never complained, never asked for wages, and never for a moment hesitated to go anywhere or to perform any act we required."

Little Maria suffered most grievously because of Ann's illness, and neither a nurse nor a drop of milk could be found in the village to make up for the loss of her usual nourishment. "Her cries in the night were heartrending," wrote Ann, "when it was impossible to supply her wants." Sometimes when the jailers were induced by presents to allow Adoniram to come out of the prison, "he carried poor little wailing Maria from door to door, still with but a few inches of chain between his shackled feet, a beggar at the breasts of pitying mothers."

Judson's release finally came, with an order to send him under escort to act as interpreter for the Burmese Army in its peace negotiations with the British. During his six weeks' absence Ann, once more in the deserted mission house in Ava, fell ill with spotted fever. In her violent delirium she did not recognize Dr. Price when he hurried to her help on the very day he was released from prison. The Burmese neighbors who crowded round her bed told him, "She is dead; and if the King of Spirits should come in, he could not recover her." But the disease was finally beaten back by the vigorous measures prescribed by Dr. Price. While still too weak to stand, she learned that her husband, whom she had not allowed to be told of her illness, had been ordered back to prison as soon as his services as interpreter were no longer required. "If I ever felt the efficacy of prayer," she said, "I did at this time. I could not rise from my couch; I could make no efforts to rescue my husband; I could only plead with that great and powerful Being who has said, 'Call upon me in the day of trouble and I will hear.' . . . I became quite composed, feeling assured that my prayers would be answered."

Once more the friendly governor came to her help. He petitioned for the release of Judson, offering himself as security. Adoniram was set free.

Hurrying through the streets of Ava as fast as his maimed feet and ankles would permit, he crept unseen into the mission house, intending to surprise Ann. A fat, half-naked Burmese woman was squatting on the floor, nursing a baby so wan and dirty that Adoniram did not recognize in her his own daughter Maria. Across the foot of the bed lay the shrunken form of his unconscious wife, a dirty cotton cap covering her head from which the glossy curls had been roughly shorn. Everything in the room bespoke ignorance and neglect. Gently Adoniram gathered the frail figure in his arms as Ann's brown eyes opened and looked into his with the dawning light of an almost unbelievable joy.

Years later Judson was present when several anecdotes were related illustrating what different men in different ages had regarded as the highest form of enjoyment derived from outward circumstances. "Pooh!" he exclaimed. "These men were not qualified to judge. I know of a much higher pleasure than that. What do you think of floating down the Irrawaddy, on a cool moonlight evening, with your wife by your side, and your baby in your arms, free—*all free?* But you cannot understand it either; it needs a twenty-one months' qualification; and I can never regret my twenty-one months of misery when I recall that one delicious thrill. I think I have had a better appreciation of what heaven may be ever since."

At the end of that blissful voyage the Judsons spent a fortnight as honored guests in the British camp. One evening at a ceremonial dinner to mark the acceptance by the Burmans of the British peace terms, several high Burmese officials were present. Imagine their dismay when the British general appeared with Ann on his arm—the white woman whom in their arrogance they had jeered at and tormented when she had appealed to them for help. Among them was the petty tyrant who had taken away her umbrella, leaving her defenseless under the fierce tropical sun. Looking round compassionately on the frightened officials, Ann spoke to them in pure, musical Burmese, telling them with a smile that they had nothing to fear from her. Perhaps they meditated on what it meant to be a Christian, for they themselves, in Ann's position, would have used their power to enjoy a sweet revenge.

In March, 1826, the Judsons returned to Rangoon and were overjoyed to meet again four of their Burmese converts and to learn that only two of the remaining fourteen had failed in loyalty to their new faith.

With hearts full of grateful thanks to God, they learned of the miraculous preservation of Judson's translation of the New Testament. The jailer who had taken the pillow had torn off its mat covering and thrown away the apparently useless hard roll that it contained. One of the Burmese converts, recognizing the roll as Judson's, though not knowing what it was, carried it away as a memento. Months later the soiled cotton covering was removed and out tumbled hundreds of sheets of priceless manuscript, unharmed.

In July, the Judsons left Rangoon to establish mission work in a province ceded to Britain after the war. Adoniram was invited to join a British embassy to Ava and to work for the inclusion of a clause in the treaty insuring religious liberty to the subjects of Burma. Ann urged him to go. Her health was apparently restored, and in her husband's absence she set eagerly to work. Each Sunday she held services for the small but loyal congregation of Burmese Christians who had accompanied them. She superintended the erection of a bamboo house and of two schoolhouses, in one of which she intended to open a school for girls. "After all our sufferings and afflictions," she wrote to Adoniram, "I cannot but hope that God has mercy and a blessing in store for us. Let us strive to obtain it by our prayers and holy life. . . . I have this day moved into the new house and for the first time since we were broken up at Ava feel myself at home."

In the midst of her cheerful, busy life, however, she was again struck down by her old enemy, jungle fever. Her constitution had been undermined by privation and suffering, and, in spite of the unremitting attention of a British doctor and army nurse, she died on October 24, 1826, at the early age of thirty-seven. The husband whose faithful and loving companion she had been for fourteen turbulent years did not even know of her death until weeks later, but the Burmese converts, for whose eternal welfare she had laid down her life, gathered like children round her bed and wept brokenheartedly for their "white mamma." A few months later poor, puny little Maria was laid by her side.

Was it worth while? Years of toil and suffering, a handful of converts, a grave in a clearing in the jungle—with such beauty, courage, charm, and unusual capacity, surely Ann Hasseltine would have used God's gifts to greater advantage in her own country.

We have our answer in Adoniram Judson's translation of the Bible, the foundation stone of the Christian church in Burma. And Adoniram could scarcely have survived his prison experiences without Ann's self-sacrificing and courageous devotion. We find it in the multiplication of those converts, so that a hundred years after Ann's death the church in Burma had one hundred and seventeen thousand Protestant members. We find it in the splendid Burmese woman, granddaughter of one of the Judsons' converts, who was one of the Burmese Christian representatives at the world meeting of the International Missionary Council at Madras in 1938.

As we brood over the life of Ann Judson, we hear the voice of her Master saying, "She hath done what she could." Indeed, we are tempted to echo the phrase used by a missionary in Manchuria about missionary wives of a later day in that tortured country, "She hath done what she could *not*." She endured and achieved to a degree that would have been impossible save for the grace of God.

Mary Moffat

MOTHER OF THE TRIBE

_M_ary Smith met her future husband, Robert Moffat, when, in 1815, he came to work for her father, a successful nursery gardener in the north of England. The young couple were between nineteen and twenty years old. It was not until Mary's father was on his way home from Manchester, where he had engaged Robert to work for him, that he bethought himself that the step he had taken might deprive him of his only daughter. For Robert had already offered himself to the London Missionary Society for service abroad, and Mary "possessed a warm missionary heart." Within a short time the young people were, indeed, deeply in love, as the father had feared; but when Robert sailed from England to the Cape in 1816, to begin his life-long missionary work among the Bechuana, Mary remained behind. They had little hope to sustain them, for Mary's parents declared that they could never consent to part with their delicate, beloved only daughter. In her self-sacrificing love for the young missionary, Mary begged Robert with tears to marry another girl who would be able to go out to the wilds of Africa as his companion. But Robert wanted only Mary, and he sailed alone, carrying in his heart the memory of her blue eyes and the delicate coloring of her girlish face demurely framed in a frilled muslin cap.

For the next two and a half years Mary lived in painful anxiety about Robert, her tender heart torn between duty to her parents and "desire to smooth the rugged path of one of those dear men who have given up all for His sake, so that through my feeble aid and assistance he may give himself more devotedly to the work." The strain was so great that she was sure she had only a few more months to live, but she continued to pray that her father and mother might be moved to give their consent to her leaving them, and in a letter to Robert's parents written in December, 1818, she was able to tell them, "I have, through the tender mercy of God, obtained permission of my dear parents to proceed, some time next spring, to join your dear son in his arduous work."

Nine months passed before Mary was able to get a passage. Her fellow travelers in the small sailing ship pronounced her the fittest person on board to go into the interior, because she bore with such unflinching calm and good temper the perils, discomforts, and discord of the three-months voyage. They did not see her as we can, through her diary, during "the silent hours of darkness when the angry billows beat against my cabin with tremendous roar; then my imagination would rove till my heart sickened and floods of tears drenched my face." She was a timid woman, as her intimate friends knew well, terrified if she met a turkey-cock; and she was on her way to face lions and savage Africans, drought and tropical thunderstorms, flooded rivers, and the nameless horrors of paganism. She wept for her mother and father, too, for neither she nor they expected to see one another again in this earthly life.

All her apprehensions and loneliness were forgotten, however, when she landed at Cape Town. Robert had traveled there to meet his bride, whose arrival "was to me nothing less than life from the dead." Mary, who had wondered whether she would find him still alive, "found him all that my heart could desire," although the worn, haggard look of his finely chiseled face and the hollowness of his dark eyes made her heart ache for all that he had suffered. In the midst of the prim nineteenth century language of Mary's diary stands the revealing phrase, "I endeavored to moderate my Robert's transports."

They were married at the end of 1819. Early in the new year, Mary accompanied her tall and powerfully built young husband some seven to eight hundred miles into the interior of Africa, and seven months after leaving her home and parents in England, she found herself at Kuruman. The journey by ox wagons, which occupied eight or nine weeks, is now accomplished in two or three days by train or in a few hours by airplane. But in interest, Mary's journey by wagon was incomparably richer than the more comfortable journey of the present day. Not that Mary found life in the wagon uncomfortable; she enjoyed it, and her letters almost suggest disappointment that on her first journey she had none of the hardships that she had steeled herself to meet! With Robert beside her, she was quite unmoved by the bluff warning of a kindly Boer farmer, "Do you know that we shot twenty-eight lions round about here last month?"

In later years, especially when she traveled with her young children, she found life in the wagon somewhat irksome. "The length of our day stages," she writes, "is about eight or twelve hours on an average, riding about three and a half miles an hour. . . . When we span out [or unyoke] a fire is immediately made, the kettle set on and coffee or tea made. . . . Having thus refreshed ourselves we have worship with our people round the fire, or in the tent which we sometimes pitch, and retire to rest in our wagons. In these we have as comfortable beds as at home, only a little narrow, especially as the family increases. . . . In every place the wolf pays us a visit and the lion is on the prowl. . . . I shall by no means attempt to prove that it is a remarkably pleasant life, for we are always heartily tired by the time the journey is done. It is at the same time a lazy and a busy life—all bustle when we stop, and unfavourable to sewing and reading when we are moving; but custom and necessity reconcile us to it."

Mary's joy at the prospect of settling in the place on which her heart had been set for several years was soon turned to bitter disappointment, for the colonial government refused them permission to remain and work at Kuruman. They returned to Griqua Town, five days' journey distant, where the London Missionary Society had been working with some success among the miscellaneous collection of Griquas, Hottentots, and Bushmen, with refugees from other tribes, which comprised its population. Here their first daughter was born, another Mary, destined to become the wife of David Livingstone. After her birth the Africans began to call Robert, Ra-Mary (father of Mary) and Mary, Ma-Mary, according to their custom of designating the parents by the name of their first-born child.

"Look what I've brought you, Mary," her husband called one day on his return from a short journey by wagon. Coming to greet him with baby Mary in her arms, his wife was astonished to see him bringing into the house two wriggling black children, who looked fearfully at the strange white woman.

"I found a party of Bushmen burying their mother," Robert explained. "They were going to bury the children alive with her, so of course I brought them to you."

"The poor little things!" Mary exclaimed, as she spoke softly to the small, frightened boy and girl. She held out her baby for them to see, and forgetting their fear, they crept nearer to the warm mother love that was ready to embrace them as well as her own child. Ann and Dicky, as the Moffats called the children, were soon part of the family, and Ann became a devoted nurse to little Mary.

Later, in 1826, they adopted another African child into their growing family, a five-weeks-old baby who was baptized Sarah. Her feeble cries had attracted their attention one morning, and Mary was "dreadfully shocked" when she found the baby, bruised and wounded, in a hole in the ground over which was a huge stone. "I took it up and brought it home, fed and washed it and dressed its wounds, to the great astonishment of the natives. They said that the mother was a rascal, but wondered much that we should love so poor an object." Probably this was the first time that some of these primitive people had ever seen in action, although without fully appreciating it, the tender love of the Good Shepherd for the lowliest and least of his little ones.

Mary's parents and friends at home were decidedly startled

to receive a letter describing her domestic life in Griqua Town, in which she warmly advocated the local custom of smearing the room floors with cow dung at least once a week. When she first saw the wife of a fellow missionary doing "this dirty trick" she resolved that she herself would never succumb to it. But before long she was finding it hard to wait with patience for Saturday, the day on which the cow dung, mixed with water, was spread as thinly as possible over the floor. "It lays the dust better than anything," she writes enthusiastically, "kills the fleas which would otherwise breed abundantly, and is a fine clear green." Still more astonishing was the decided preference she expressed for entertaining the local chief after he had scoured his hands thoroughly with a piece of cow dung than when he sat down to a meal with his hands covered with the fat and red ochre with which the Africans of that region smeared their bodies.

Eventually permission came from the government for the Moffats to settle at Kuruman, which was to be their home for the next forty-seven years. The settlement depended for its existence on the water of the Kuruman River, a mere channel for the greater part of its course.

Conditions at Kuruman were far from encouraging. "Could we but see the smallest fruit, we could rejoice amidst the privations and toils which we bear," Mary wrote in 1822. For five years missionaries had been working among the people, but not one soul treated them with anything but ridicule and contempt. The Bechuana stole their crops, their sheep, their calves, their tools, and household implements; they encroached upon their gardens, which they had irrigated at the cost of immense labor; they even stole loaves from the oven, if Mary turned her back for a few minutes. In the constant warfare between the tribes all sides were guilty of shocking barbarities. We can feel Mary's shudder when she writes of some of the Bechuana having been forced by hunger into cannibalism. "In the natives of South Africa," she writes, "there is nothing naturally engaging; their extreme selfishness, filthiness, obstinate stupidity and want of sensibility have a tendency to disgust, and sometimes cause the mind to shrink from the idea of spending the whole life among them, far from every tender and endearing circle." But, having thus expressed her natural feelings, she is filled with contrition and begs her friends to pray that she may be more ready to follow the example of her Master. Seven more painful years were to pass before the missionaries received any encouragement.

Robert and Mary were sitting at breakfast one morning. A group of Africans, smeared with red ochre and grease, trooped through the open doorway, bringing a vile smell with them, to stare at the white folks who made such a business of eating. A table with a cloth on it, knives, forks, spoons, plates, cups and saucers! What was the matter with fingers and a calabash and a seat on Mother Earth? Ma-Mary too, they noticed, sat at the table with her husband, instead of humbly serving him in the African way and being thankful for the scraps he might leave. The young couple at the table were so used to being stared at that they scarcely noticed the jostling onlookers or heard the interminable discussion about their queer ways, although Mary sighed as she saw that her clean walls and furniture were again suffering from contact with greasy African bodies.

"Robert," said Mary, "do you remember the day when I asked our friends to leave us alone while we had a meal and they threatened to throw a brick at me? I didn't realize then how very rude I'd been, according to African ideas of hospitality. Now I've learned to give them a welcome whenever they come and however much dirt they bring into the house with them."

"It hasn't been easy, Mary, I know that. You are a wonderful homemaker though, in spite of every obstacle, and a home in these savage surroundings is like a green oasis in the desert."

She smiled, then said, "By the way, Robert, I've answered Mrs Greaves's letter from Sheffield. Mine can go to the coast at the next opportunity. You remember she asked whether she could send us out something that would be useful for the mission. Well, I've asked her for a communion service."

"A communion service!" Robert repeated with painful intensity. "Mary, dear, we haven't a single convert, nor the prospect of one, and the mission board is becoming so discouraged that they talk of closing this station. Why do you think we shall need communion vessels, of all things?"

"We shall need them some day, Robert. Perhaps we may not live to see it, but the awakening will come as surely as the sun will rise tomorrow. Our covenant God has promised us. Do you not believe his promises?"

"Bless you, my dear," he murmured. "You will never let us lose hope. In spite of your delicate body and your headaches, and those black fits of depression that you have to fight, you are stronger in faith than any of us big, healthy men. What should we have done without you in these dark years? You have saved us from despair again and again by your courage and your unconquerable faith."

"Perhaps it is because I am so weak and fearful that I know I have no strength in myself. I have to trust Him or I should die. But I have a hard fight sometimes, Robert. I felt frightened enough when the people threatened to burn us in our beds because they believed we had driven the rain away. And that terrible day when the chief and his twelve attendants came to warn us to leave the country. My heart felt like ice when the chief balanced the great spear in his hand, pointing it at you. But you didn't flinch, Robert. I can see you now, flinging your arms wide as if to welcome the spear and crying out in your deep voice, 'If you want to get rid of us, you must resort to stronger measures than that, because our hearts are with you.' Do you remember?"

"Yes. They didn't seem to know what to do then, did they? I remember the chief said to the others, 'They must have ten lives if they are so fearless of death,' and he lowered his spear as if he knew it was useless. . . . Perhaps you are right, Mary, and we shall need that communion service after all."

Three years after that conversation the communion plate, sent by Mrs. Greaves, arrived at Kuruman on the day before the one set apart for the celebration of Holy Communion in which the first six baptized converts of the mission were to take part.

The great awakening came in 1829, nearly ten years after Mary had landed in South Africa. It was a spontaneous turning toward the gospel by people who had maintained for years a stolid indifference to the missionaries' message, although they were willing enough to accept the material benefits that the white men brought. The tremendous emotional tide ebbed after a time, but many converts had been made, and these grew in maturity. With their own hands they built a schoolhouse and a church, under Moffat's direction. Taking as his motto, "The Bible and the plow for Africa," Robert set himself the almost superhuman task of reducing the language of his people to writing, and then translating the Bible into it. This was his work for many years. Far into each night he toiled, for during the day he labored on the land under the burning African sun. Gradually he was able to impart his own skill as a gardener to the Bechuana, who learned to grow crops of wheat, barley, peas, carrots, and potatoes by the aid of irrigation. He introduced the plow, driven by the men, in place of the primitive pickax used as a hoe by the women. Until now agriculture had been considered beneath the dignity of men. Instead of living in a state of idleness and semi-starvation, at times reduced to cannibalism by hunger, the Bechuana became industrious and well fed. Robert also taught the men to read and write, to work as carpenters and smiths, and to use the printing press that he himself made.

The women, too, wanted to learn. Mary showed them how to bathe their babies and helped them to understand why their children were so often ill and what remedies to use. She helped them to prepare the kind of food that small children should eat, and gave them motherly lectures on the benefits of discipline and regular hours in bringing up a family. Her counsels were the more effective because of the example she gave in rearing her own little brood. By 1831 the Moffats had five children of their own, in addition to the small Africans whom they had taken into the family. Five more children were born to them later.

The African women began to want clothes like Mary's and had no idea how to make them. So Mary started a sewing class and cut out simple garments for them to wear at their baptism and at church on Sundays. How relieved she was when her visitors began to wash themselves and put on clean dresses, instead of smearing themselves all over with red ochre and smelly grease! She hardly knew whether to laugh or cry when she saw the African women's clumsy fingers trying to hold the slippery little needles. Having had to do the field work, they were more accustomed to the feel of a pickax than the delicate little implement, which was always eluding them. Mary's patience was sorely tried, too, when one of her pupils put a garment together anyhow, and another sewed hers up like a pillow cover and then wondered why she could not get into it!

When Mary's eldest daughter was fourteen her mother decided that, in spite of all the difficulties and dangers, she and her younger brother and sister must be taken to the Cape to school. These three—Mary, Ann, and Robert—were already at the Wesleyan school near Grahamstown, to which she had taken them in 1830, for "keeping them at home is beyond all doubt highly improper," she wrote to her father. The viciousness of a pagan environment made it dangerous for boys and girls approaching adolescence.

So in 1835 Mary set off with her three youngest children in the wagon, to fetch the others from the Wesleyan school, take them all to Port Elizabeth, and there see the three eldest off on the somewhat dangerous eleven days' passage by sailing ship to the Cape. For the mother, making this arduous journey without Robert's stalwart help and affectionate solicitude, those seven months on trek were a trial of faith. On the way south they found the Orange River a raging torrent, and "I was compelled to lie on the banks of that mighty stream for one round month." Mary had had a severe illness earlier in the year, after which her health had steadily declined, and she suffered a great deal from the extreme heat in that exposed position. At last she decided to join some Boer travelers who were making preparations to cross on a raft. Eighteen wagons went over "that frightful river" in three days, without accident, on a raft made of four or five willow trees tied underneath with bark, with two or three trees tied crosswise underneath. It was drawn across from one bank to the other, over eighty yards of "tremendously deep water," by ropes made of bullock's hide. At the point where Mary had waited so long, hoping to be able to cross, the river was five hundred yards wide.

The Orange River had again to be crossed on the return journey of Mary and the three little ones from Port Elizabeth to Kuruman; but by then it was fordable with wagons, though still very high. In order to replenish their stocks at Kuruman, Mary had bought sheep and cows from Boer farmers along the way, and these were a formidable addition to her cares. Imagine her delight when Robert met her at the last farmhouse close to the river and she was able to resign into his kindly and capable hands the direction of the delicate operation of crossing the river with their train of wagons and domestic animals.

Toward the end of 1838 the whole Moffat family started for Cape Town. Robert's health had suffered severely under the strain of constant translation work. Sometimes, Mary told her father, he became so overdone with mental exercise that he passed whole nights, with the exception of an hour or two, in restless tossings. Mary herself, always delicate, suffered more and more from physical weakness, and for both of them a change from Kuruman was necessary. Moffat, too, had by this time completed his Herculean task of translating the whole of the New Testament into Sechuana, and the printing press that he had set up at Kuruman was not equal to the task of printing it. In Cape Town, however, they discovered to their dismay that even there no printing firm was equipped to undertake book printing on the scale required. It was plain that the work would have to be done in England, and Moffat and his family embarked on a small ship with wretched accommodations, carrying troops on the way from China.

After they were aboard, but before the ship had actually sailed out of Table Bay, Mary gave birth to a daughter. Sailing within a few hours, they ran into weather so severe, with contrary winds, that all the passengers and many of the ship's company were prostrate with seasickness. The Moffats' six-year-old son was taken violently ill with dysentery. Mary could not rise from her bunk, and Robert and the others of the family were unable to overcome their nausea sufficiently to attend to him. He lay beside his mother, who tried in her own weakness to comfort him. When the new baby was three days old her brother died. For days the distracted parents despaired of the life of another of their children, but within two or three weeks the weather moderated and all the others recovered. After nearly three months of this sad and tedious voyage, Mary was thankful to set foot on shore with the children early in 1839, although her husband shrank from landing in what had become to him a strange country.

Robert longed to see the Sechuana New Testament through the press and then to slip away again to South Africa before the winter. But they were not able to leave England until the beginning of 1843, so great was the demand for Moffat as a speaker. Their visit to England coincided with a great wave of missionary enthusiasm, and he was hurried by coach from town to town all over England and Scotland, to satisfy the popular clamor to see and hear this man with the splendid physique and magnificent voice who spoke so earnestly and convincingly about the growing work in what was still thought of as the heart of the Dark Continent of Africa.

Mary, too, felt homesick for Africa, in spite of her joy in the companionship of her father and old and new friends. Writing to their fellow missionary in Kuruman she says, "I long to get home. I fear I shall forget what I knew of the language. I long to see the spot again where we have so long toiled and suffered, to see our beloved companions in the toil and suffering, and to behold our swarthy brothers and sisters again; and I long for my own home, for though loaded with the kindness of friends, and welcome everywhere, still home is homely!" Mary was unable to accompany Robert on his deputation journeys, as she was busy with her two little daughters born since the family left South Africa. The older children, also, claimed a large share of her attention, especially since the boys were to be left behind to attend school in England.

In April, 1843, the Moffats and a number of new missionaries landed at Cape Town, and "soon the old familiar scene presented itself: the long train of ox-wagons, winding over hill and down dale, sticking fast in muddy fords and making fifteen or twenty miles a day." When they were a hundred and fifty miles from Kuruman they were met by David Livingstone, one of Moffat's recruits, who had preceded them to Africa. Each succeeding day they were met by other groups of joyous friends, both missionaries and Africans, always with fresh teams of oxen, until, as the party drew near to Kuruman, it resembled a royal progress. The long cavalcade reached the Moffats' home at Kuruman shortly before dawn. Crowds of their African "children" were there to greet them, even at that hour, and for weeks afterwards many came from long distances around to show their joy in the return of their beloved Ra-Mary and Ma-Mary, whom they had begun to fear they would never see again.

Robert's joy in the homecoming shines through his first letter to the London Missionary Society: "The well-known sound of the church-going bell in the Kuruman vale again salutes the ear. The substantial chapel and the mission-houses, and the tall Babylonian willows waving in the breeze, the swallows skimming aloft, having returned from the warm tropics, the buzz of a hundred infant-school children at this moment pouring out for a minute's play, some chanting over again what they have just been singing, others romping and running about on the greensward—are sights and sounds pleasant and melodious to eye and ear."

With the coming of new missionaries and the opening of several new stations at distances of a hundred to two hundred miles, Kuruman took on more and more the character of a bridgehead. Mary had her hands full in entertaining the missionaries and their wives when they came to Kuruman to report to Moffat and consult with him. They came to her for counsel and encouragement, for help in sickness, and for supplies of food and comforts.

Among her many patients were a French missionary whom she nursed through smallpox and an African wounded by a buffalo, as well as her husband when he came in one day with the blood pouring from a long jagged cut in his arm, which had been caught in the mill while Robert was grinding their flour. Mary's motherliness took no account of racial or national boundaries.

Out of her own experience as a pioneer in even more difficult and discouraging circumstances, Mary was always ready
to sympathize with the missionaries and their African assist-
ants and to give them practical help and advice. As she
became more frail she was unable to take such an active part
as she had taken at first in the work of the mission, but to
missionaries and African Christians alike she was the mother
to whom they turned at all times, sure of her sympathy and
loving interest.

Once, when Mary playfully remarked to a friend, "Robert
can never say that I have hindered him in his work," her
husband replied quickly with the familiar twinkle in his eye,
"She has often sent me away from house and home for months
together for evangelistic purposes and in my absence has
managed the station as well or better than I could have done
it myself!" In telling this reminiscence to one of the Moffats'
sons, the friend to whom his parents had made these remarks
commented, "She was indeed a missionary second only to
himself."

Mary always remembered one particular day as among the
happiest days of her long and busy life. A little group of
African Christian women, in clean cotton dresses in place of
the red ochre and grease that had formerly covered their
bodies, came to the mission house and asked her to teach
them to make candles. In the Bechuana villages no artificial
lighting of any kind was known, and as soon as the sun had
set and the last red embers of the cooking fires had fallen into
gray ash the people were forced to sit in their huts in complete darkness.

"But now," said the spokesman of the group to Mary,
"Ra-Mary has taught our husbands to read and he has printed

Bibles and hymns for us. We want to be able to see to read them in the evenings after our work is done."

So Mary gladly showed them how she made candles to light the mission house, by pouring fat into molds with a piece of rag for a wick. Soon little points of light shining through the darkness from African huts gave the Moffats new cause for rejoicing.

"The gospel is really taking root among them now, Robert," his wife whispered, as they stood for a few minutes outside the hut of one of the elders of the church and heard his family heartily singing a Christian hymn.

"Yes, my dear. Christ is bringing real home life to Africa, and you have helped him to do it here."

James Chapman, an explorer and trader who accompanied Robert in 1854 on his second visit to the warlike Matabele people, whose savage chief, Umsiligazi, revered and loved Moffat, gives a picture of life at Kuruman that dramatizes the changes made in thirty years or so: "With the Moffats we were never in any want of milk, new bread, and fresh butter. There was never any lack of grapes, apples, peaches, and all other products of the garden. All we see is the result of well directed labors. The natives here are the most enlightened and civilized I have seen, the greater portion wearing clothes and being able to read and write. It was pleasant on Sunday to see them, neatly and cleanly clad, going to church."

And William Oswell, the friend and companion of David Livingstone on some of his journeys, writes of his visit to Kuruman: "How well I remember the exquisite arrangement and order of the mother's household, the affectionate interest in the wayfarers, the father's courtly hospitality and kindly advice. . . . Dear old Kuruman! My short visits to you were among the happiest in my life; no little kingdom ever had a better king and queen, no home a better host and hostess."

On Sunday, the twentieth of March, 1870, Mary watched her Robert mount for the last time into the pulpit of the church that he had toiled to build at Kuruman. They were both seventy-five, and each had given rather more than fifty years of service to Africa. Mary still thought her husband the handsomest man she had known as he lifted his fine head, straightened his broad shoulders, and gazed benignly under shaggy eyebrows at the rows upon rows of dusky men, women, and children, whom they must leave behind in a few days' time when they began their last journey to England. Always delicate, Mary was a frail little old lady now. Her apple-blossom bloom had faded, but her blue eyes still shone with the sweet and serious sincerity that had won Robert's heart so many years ago. In all that great congregation very few were their contemporaries. The older people had been children, for the most part, when the Moffats came among them, and their children and grandchildren knew little of the life of degradation, want, and ignorance from which Robert and Mary Moffat, with "the gospel and the plow," had rescued the Bechuana.

A few days later the last farewells were said and the old couple passed reluctantly through the door of the house in which they had lived for forty years. They were not leaving Africa to go home; they were leaving home to go to England. As they walked to their wagon "they were beset by the crowds, each longing for one more touch of the hand and one more word; and as the wagon drove away it was followed by all who could walk, and a long and pitiful wail arose, enough to melt the hardest heart." Mary's care for her African children was active to the end. During the last few moments she spent with her son, John, who was left in charge of the mission station, she pleaded for a man who was in deep disgrace for his conduct toward Moffat.

Mary survived but a few months after being transplanted to England. Robert's first exclamation when her death left him bowed down with sorrow told the secret of her influence in his life: "For fifty-three years I have had her to pray for me."

Mary Livingstone

"THE MAIN SPOKE IN MY WHEEL"

David Livingstone, that rugged young Scottish missionary doctor, who went to Africa in 1841, seemed determined to remain unmarried. Writing to a friend on the subject two years later, he remarked with a wry humor, "There's no outlet for me when I begin to think of getting married but that of sending home an advertisement to the *Evangelical Magazine,* and, if I get very old, it must be for some decent sort of widow. In the meantime," continued the downright young man, "I am too busy to think of anything of the kind." Within two years he was married; so much for masculine self-sufficiency! His bride was no "decent sort of widow" either, but charming, twenty-three-year-old Mary Moffat; he himself was thirty-one. It was fitting that David's first meeting in Africa with his "Queen of the Wagon" should be in her father's wagon when the Moffat family were returning from their only furlough in England in the spring of 1843.

David had heard Robert Moffat speak, at a meeting in London, of his experiences in South Africa. With burning eloquence the broad-shouldered, full-bearded veteran won Livingstone for Africa when he swept his arm in a spacious gesture, crying, "I have sometimes seen the smoke of a thousand villages where no missionary has ever been."

A few months before the Moffats returned to Africa, David had been badly mauled by a lion and had spent his convalescence at Kuruman. He rode out a hundred and fifty miles to meet the returning missionaries and came to Kuruman with them. During the weeks that followed, he found it dangerously sweet to tell such a sympathetic and discriminating listener as the younger Mary about his work at Mabotsa (did he remind her that the name means "a marriage feast"?), and to watch her at work among the African boys and girls in the infants' school. He, too, as he told her, had started a school, "to which the poor little naked things came with fear and trembling. The women make us the hobgoblins of their children, telling them that the white men bite children and feed them with dead men's brains, and all manner of nonsense."

One day, under the great spreading branches of the almond tree that Robert Moffat had planted, David spoke to Mary of his love and she responded with an ardor and sincerity that matched his own. No shadow of future separation saddened their engagement, for at that time David believed that his missionary life would be passed at Mabotsa, doing work similar to that of Robert Moffat. If by that time he had heard God's call to his future life-work of exploration in Africa, perhaps he would have lacked the courage to ask Mary to marry him. But his self-sacrifice would have failed in its object of sparing Mary unhappiness. She was the stuff of which heroes' wives are made, and even if she could have seen into the future, with all its separation and hardships, she would still gladly have married this man and given him the sustaining power of her unfaltering love and faith.

Mary Moffat said of her daughter that she was less openly pious than other members of the family, but that she was a very practical Christian. "Accept me, Lord, as I am and make me such as thou wouldst have me to be," was the private prayer that her husband found among her papers after her death.

David Livingstone took his bride, after their marriage in January, 1845, to a stone-and-brick house that he had built mainly with his own hands. As he showed her round it he proudly exclaimed, "There, my dear, every brick and every stick was put square with my own right hand." Perhaps the primitive housekeeping on which she entered was not quite so difficult for her as it had been at first for that other Mary, her mother, for Mary Livingstone had been born and brought up in Africa, although much of her life had been spent at a city school and some years of it in England. Everything they needed—bread, butter, candles, soap—they had to make from the raw materials. "But," wrote David, happy in his enjoyment of home life for the first time in many years, "there is not much hardship in being almost entirely dependent on ourselves; and married life is all the sweeter when so many comforts emanate directly from the thrifty, striving housewife's hands."

Their first months of married life were saddened by painful

differences between Livingstone and his senior fellow missionary at Mabotsa, who wrote to the directors of the London Missionary Society that he refused to be made any longer an "appendix" to a younger man. This older man worked well in a humdrum fashion, and hotly resented the daring initiative and assumption of leadership by his young colleague. Rather than allow strained relations between the missionaries to become a stumbling block to the Africans whom they were trying to influence, David and Mary decided, with characteristic generosity, to give up their house and school and garden and start another station some distance from Mabotsa. Out of a salary of five hundred dollars a year it was not easy to build another new house, and in asking the missionary society for a building grant of a hundred and fifty dollars, David was compelled, against his will, to speak of the hardships of their first two years together: "We endured for a long while, but when our corn was done, we were fairly obliged to go to Kuruman for supplies. I can bear what other Europeans would consider hunger and thirst without inconvenience, but when we arrived, to hear the old women who had seen my wife depart about two years before exclaiming, 'Bless me, how lean she is! Has he starved her? Is there no food in the country to which she has been?' was more than I could well bear."

Having built another house and school, Mary and David settled down to help the Bakwena people. After family worship and breakfast between 6 and 7 A.M., they both taught in the school, men and women as well as children being invited to learn. School was over at eleven, and then Mary attended to her many home duties, while David worked as smith, carpenter, or gardener. "We came nearly," he wrote, "to what may be considered as indispensable in the accomplishments of a missionary family in Africa, that is, the husband to be a jack-of-all-trades without-doors and the wife a maid-of-all-work within." After dinner and an hour's rest in the worst heat of the day, Mary gathered her infants' school together. The children, who were left by their parents entirely to their own devices, attended the classes with gusto, and sometimes Mary was confronted by as many as eighty wide-eyed, chocolate-brown, squirming youngsters. On some afternoons she held sewing classes for the girls of the village, where they learned far more than sewing from their gentle teacher. These classes were as well attended and relished as the infants' school. David, meanwhile, was talking to the men and visiting and prescribing for those who were sick. In the evenings they held public services of worship and classes of instruction in the Christian faith. Mary taught the women and girls and David the men and boys.

The exercise of rigid discipline for moral lapses among their converts was the heaviest and most painful duty that had fallen upon the Moffats; and in their turn David and Mary found that missionaries must be stern and uncompromising in the life-and-death struggle that they initiate between Christianity and the moral laxity of pagan society. Their hearts were sore when they discovered that the chief, Sechele, one of their first converts, and the families of the native teachers, had been guilty of gross sins while still maintaining their profession of Christianity.

"And the worst of it is, Mary," David said, pouring out the painful story into her sympathetic ears, "the whole town knows what their conduct has been. We are the only ones who were kept in ignorance, and I have been administering the Sacrament to them as consistent believers. It will do great harm to our cause here, I'm afraid. Oh, Mary, how terrible the forces of heathenism which we have to fight! How can you and I in a few short years expect to do anything to change the evil customs of generations of unchecked savagery?"

Mary knew that David was on the point of being enveloped in one of his fits of Gaelic gloom. "But you and I are not fighting alone, dear," she reminded him quietly. "And even though our people do lapse, at any rate now they know that they are sinning and are ashamed. Isn't it a miracle that Sechele was ready to put away all his wives but one, even though he hasn't yet been able to live up to the new standard? We must be patient with them, David, even as God is patient with us."

"What should I do without your wise counsel and encouragement, Mary?" he replied. "And I am convinced that the very fact of your being here and setting them such a shining example of simple goodness and purity is worth much more than all my exhortations."

A terrible drought led the Bakwena people to move their village some distance away, and the Livingstones went with them to Kolobeng, where they built yet another house and school. This was the last real home that Mary and David were to have together in all the seventeen years of their marriage.

While still at Mabotsa the Africans had begun to call Mary Ma-Robert, to indicate that she was the proud mother of a son, the first white baby they had ever seen. In the autumn of 1846, between the birth of Robert and of her second child, Agnes, the following year, Mary was gladdened by a visit from her mother, that indomitable middle-aged pioneer, with her three youngest children, who were eager to inspect their first nephew. The older woman knew from experience the loneliness and hardships of the frontier missionary's wife, and she braved the arduous and dangerous journey without her husband, who could not leave Kuruman, for the sake of her eldest child. Mary Moffat and her family were escorted by a native hunting party and were about three weeks on trek to the Livingstones' station. A seasoned wagon traveler, she passed lightly over the difficulties of finding water, of wagons stuck fast in the mud, of persistent danger from lions. Mary welcomed her mother with tears of relief and joy, and was lifted by her sturdy faith and practical help over a period of physical weakness and spiritual despondency.

It was plain to Mary Moffat that David and her daughter were very much in love. Indeed, with her more rigid up-bringing, she sometimes wondered whether, in their joy in each other's company, they were not almost too playful and merry for missionaries surrounded by heathen tribes perishing for the gospel; although she assured herself that, except in the intimacy of family life, they were both extremely quiet and reserved. In spite of this picture of happy home life, however, she was already visited by those misgivings, which she expressed so strongly a little later, as to whether David should have married at all, when she heard him talk with such intensity of longing of the journeys of exploration that he wished to undertake. For by this time the fever that was in Livingstone's blood could not be denied. All the time he felt the pressure on his spirit of the vast regions beyond, which lay untouched while all the missionary forces remained within the boundary of South Africa. He dreamed of opening a way for the gospel among these unreached tribes and then of leaving African Christian missionaries among them to carry on the work.

After the longest of his journeys so far, he came back to Mary full of thrilling news of his first great geographical discovery. He had been accompanied by William Oswell, the English hunter and explorer, who had generously provided the guides and much of the equipment for the trip, and who eventually became one of their closest friends.

"Africa isn't all desert, as everyone has thought," David told Mary on his return. Like Othello he could have said of his Desdemona, "She loved me for the dangers I had passed, and I loved her that she did pity them."

"Mary, I have seen a great lake called Ngami, its shining waters stretching far out of sight. And the Africans there talk of a country full of rivers and large trees beyond. Next year I shall start out again, and I want you and the bairns to come with me. Mary, will you come with me? I am always lonely without you by my side."

Robert, Agnes, and even little Thomas, the youngest child, knew that there was some exciting adventure in the wind. They were forever asking, "When do we start in the wagon, Mamma?" Mary looked at them a little sadly, but she only answered, "When Papa is ready," although in her heart she dreaded the day when she and David would set out across the trackless, waterless desert with three small children in their keeping.

In April, 1850, they set out from Kolobeng, their third home in five brief years of marriage—the "Queen of the Wagon" and her three children, Livingstone, and a small company of Africans with a long train of wagons. Sechele, the Bakwena chief, and some of his people traveled with them.

David's daring plan was to form a new mission settlement far to the north, in the country of Chief Sebituane, of whom he had heard but had never met. Mary's mother and father were against the plan. They felt that he had already moved too often, and that he should stay at Kolobeng to consolidate his work there. They were quite sure that, at any rate, he should discover a suitable place for the new settlement before taking Mary and the children with him.

No doubt David was too impetuous in thus exposing his family to danger. His friend Oswell had gone to the Cape to get equipment and had promised to make the further attempt with him; the cooperation of this seasoned traveler and the supplies that his money was able to provide would have lessened materially the discomfort and danger to Mary and their little family. But David was too eager to wait.

Day merged into night and night into day during that seemingly endless journey across the desert, eight hundred and seventy miles from their home at Kolobeng. They suffered from lack of meat; sympathetic Africans often brought the children a kind of large caterpillar, which they relished, and a very large frog, which looked like chicken when it was cooked. A dish of locusts, too, was quite a treat; strongly vegetable in flavor, the taste of their flesh varied with the plants on which they fed.

Near the lake they met a party of English big game hunters. One of their number had already died of fever, but the others recovered in response to the care lavished on them by the Livingstones. David spent hours talking with the local chief, who reluctantly allowed himself to be propitiated by the white man—at the price of Livingstone's rifle, a valuable gift from a friend, which he could not replace.

"You and the children are doing a wonderful missionary work, Mary," he assured her, when he returned from one of those interviews with the chief. "Your presence inspires the Africans with confidence. They are sure that if I meant any harm, I shouldn't have come cumbered by a wife and children. The chief has promised to protect and feed you and the little ones and to give me provisions to go on farther to visit Sebituane, the chief I have long wished to meet."

If Mary's heart sank at the thought of being left alone with this unknown tribe, with no skilled help or conveniences of any kind if she and the children were ill, she did not utter her fears. She had not seen Lake Ngami, the discovery of which had meant so much to her husband, as she had had her hands full, nursing the fever-stricken patients and caring for the children, while she herself was far from well. David took her on a special six-mile trip to the lake with the children the day before he was to leave for his visit with Sebituane. On the margin of the lake David lifted the children from the wagon. With squeals of delight they rushed into the water, paddling and playing in it like ducklings. Side by side their mother and father stood watching them and thanked God in their hearts that he had brought them so far in safety, despite the dangers of wild beasts, fever, famine, the risk of drought, and unfriendly Africans. That night two of the children were burning with fever, and the African bearers were attacked also. Evidently the neighborhood of David's beautiful lake was unhealthy, and he could not leave Mary and the children there. Nor could he take them any farther with him into the unknown territory. Instead of exploring farther he was forced to order an immediate retreat. They hurried back to the less pleasant but healthier desert, and so home to Kolobeng. There their fourth child, Elizabeth, was soon born, "a sweet little girl with blue eyes," but she died in the late autumn of 1850 at the age of six weeks.

This sorrow, coming after the hardships and strain of the long journey, broke down Mary's resistance, and she was seriously ill. The right side of her face and head was paralyzed, and from that time on she was periodically threatened with partial paralysis. David took her to Kuruman, where her mother nursed her, and her sisters delightedly played with their young nephews and niece.

Probably it was the remembrance of her daughter, so wan and weak after this first long jouney, that prompted Mary Moffat to write a letter of the strongest protest to her son-in-law when she learned that he was preparing to start off again with Mary and the children. She reminded him of the death of baby Elizabeth and of Mary's grave illness, and "in the name of everything that was just, kind, and even decent," besought him "to abandon an arrangement which all the world would condemn." The fact that Mary's fifth child was born five months after the second expedition started, and while they were still on the move, gives startling point to her mother's indignant protest.

No remonstrances, however, availed to turn David from his inflexible purpose. If anything could have done so, it would have been his deep love for Mary and their young children, but his lofty sense of duty moved him above all other considerations. With Mary, and when alone, he spent many hours in prayer asking for specific guidance. "I am convinced," he told his wife, "that it is our duty to go out together to seek a new station for the gospel in Sebituane's country. God will take care of us if we are doing our duty," he continued tenderly, "and it is better to trust in the Lord than put confidence in man." His strongest advocate was Mary's love for her fearless, almost frighteningly determined husband. She longed above everything else to be with him, and she shared his sense of a divine mission. He upheld her by his strong, simple faith in the overarching providence of God; and the utter confidence with which she put her life and the lives of their children in his care nerved him to fresh endeavor.

In April, 1851, they set off again, this time accompanied by William Oswell, who felt deeply the responsibility of having a woman and children in the caravan. He and his men went ahead to dig wells so that Mary and her little family would be sure of having water. In doing so he risked his own life, and on one occasion nearly lost it when he was attacked by an infuriated lioness.

They followed the old route, but their Bushman guide lost his way in a naïve attempt to save his legs from being wounded by thorn bushes.

Four days crawled slowly by. The silence of the desert was menacing, for no living creature could exist long in the midst of that desolation.

"Mary," her husband said quietly one afternoon, "this is the driest desert I have ever seen. No water even when we dig deep into the sand. We must use the water we have in the wagon very sparingly until we can get more."

Pale to the lips, she replied, "The cask has leaked and there is scarcely a drop of water left."

Already burning with thirst, the children were crying miserably, as each saw the terrible fear in the eyes of the other the husband and wife lifted their souls in prayer. If they did not reach water soon, their children would die before their eyes. Mary uttered no word of reproach, though David could not meet the dumb anguish in her eyes.

On the afternoon of the fifth day, when all seemed lost, they were startled by a shout. One of the men who had gone ahead had found a muddy hole containing a little brackish water. The mother and father watched their suffering children quench their burning thirst and then moistened their own parched and blackened lips. The small quantity of dirty water gathered in that hole saved the lives of all in the party.

Farther and farther north they traveled, beyond Lake Ngami to the country of the warlike chief, Sebituane, whom David had longed to meet. The African chief, indomitable, courageous, and governed by lofty purpose, shared some of Livingstone's qualities. The two men became close friends, and Sebituane offered him a piece of land on which to build a house and start a mission. Within a few weeks, however, the chief was taken ill and died. His daughter ruled in his place, and she, too, was friendly to the white travelers. Leaving Mary and the children in the care of the headmen of the district, David and William Oswell traveled on until they discovered the mighty and beautiful river that they afterwards learned was the Zambezi. They could not, however, find any district sufficiently free from fever and other disadvantages to make it possible for a white missionary to settle there with his family.

While Mary was alone among the pagan African tribesmen ruled by Sebituane's daughter, the children were repeatedly ill with fever. When David returned and learned that his gallant Mary, herself ill, had feared that the children might die in his absence, he was ready to yield to Oswell's persuasions not to expose them to further risks. They set off again on the weary trek back to Kolobeng, but before they arrived there a son, their fifth child, whom thev named William Oswell, was born, in September, 1851, at a place that they called Bellevue.

The sufferings of his wife and family on this journey finally convinced David that he had no right to take them with him on any further journeys, especially as he was already possessed by the daring plan of finding a road to the sea, either to the east or the west coast, so that legitimate commerce could enter Africa and replace the horrors of the slave trade. Much would thus be done to prepare the way for Christian missions, which, he was convinced, could never thrive while Africa was closed to the outside world.

After long and prayerful talks they decided that Mary should take the children home to Britain for two or three years. "For though I may be justified in risking my own life in the service of our Master, I may not use the same freedom with your life and the lives of the children," David pointed out. "But how shall I get on without you, my dear? And to let the children go will be like tearing out my bowels. If only," he added wistfully, "I were able to settle down to a quiet, peaceful life among the Bakwena or some other small tribe, how thankful I should be! We should be together, and I could devote some of my time to the children. But Providence seems to call me to the regions beyond, and I dare not refuse to go."

She who had always understood him understood him now, and his heart did homage to her unselfish love and noble faith. Together they traveled by wagon to the Cape, and in

April, 1852, Mary and the four children sailed for home. Both she and David knew that they might never meet again, and their hearts were torn with anguish. Mary's was the harder lot, for she was now the sole guardian of the children and could do nothing but wait and pray for David's safety. Frequent letters came from him at first, but the intervals grew longer and longer as he plunged farther into unknown country. One letter, which he wrote soon after saying good-by in Cape Town, seemed to her like the warm clasp of his hand as she read with blurred eyes his declaration of undying love:

MY DEAREST MARY—

How I miss you now, and the dear children! You have been a great blessing to me. May God bless you for all your kindnesses. I see no face now to be compared with that sunburnt one which has so often greeted me with its kind looks. You may read the letters over again that I wrote at Mabotsa, the sweet time you know. . . . I never show all my feelings, but I can truly say, my dearest, that I loved you when I married you, and the longer I lived with you I loved you the better. . . . Take the children round you and kiss them for me. Tell them I have left them for the love of Jesus, and they must love Him too.

Poor Mary! A stranger in England, without a home to call her own, with four children to whom she must be both mother and father, her health shattered by hardship and the birth of five children in six years, and full of terrible apprehensions about her husband. Those who had known her as "Queen of the Wagon" as it rolled over the African desert would scarcely have known her for the same woman in England. What was there in common between the winsome girl who was the life and soul of those African expeditions, making arrangements for the comfort and safety of the travelers and keeping up their spirits with her merry laughter and quiet faith, and the reserved, sad-eyed woman whose fear blotted out for a time even the face of God? In the darkness, however, she clung to the habit of prayer, and her serenity returned even before she heard, after a long, hard silence, of her husband's safety.

Four and a half years after they parted in Cape Town she traveled to meet him at Southampton. With the light returning to her eye and the bloom to her cheek, she gave him shyly some verses she had written for him. Their simple pathos, enhanced by the halting rhythm, told him more of what she had endured than a thousand letters:

> *A hundred thousand welcomes! How my heart is gushing o'er*
> *With the love and joy and wonder thus to see your face once more.*
> *How did I live without you these long, long years of woe?*
> *It seems as if 'twould kill me to be parted from you now.*
> *Do you think I would reproach you with the sorrow that I bore*
> *Since the sorrow is all over, now I have you here once more?*
> *And there's nothing but the gladness and the love within my heart,*
> *And the hope so sweet and certain that again we'll never part.*

That Christmas of 1856 was a merry one for Mary and the children. David, with his spare figure and deeply furrowed, weather-beaten face, was now a famous man, but he was still his wife's lover and the children thought him the best playfellow and storyteller in the world.

During the following two years Mary accompanied her husband to countless gatherings where he was fêted as one of the greatest discoverers and scientists of the age. She knew that he was utterly sincere when he insisted always that he was a simple missionary, whose only concern was to open up Africa to Christianity. Everywhere he went he made an earnest appeal for missionaries, the most famous being the words, electrifying to his hearers, with which he ended a lecture in the senate house at Cambridge: "I beg to direct your attention to Africa. . . . I go back to Africa to try to make an open path for commerce and Christianity; do you carry out the work which I have begun. I leave it with you!"

At some of these meetings Mary blushed to hear herself praised. She treasured the words of Lord Shaftesbury as, with measured courtesy, he told, at a reception given in her husband's honor, of her part in David's triumphs. "She cheered the early part of our friend's career by her spirit, her counsel and her society. . . . She passed many years with her children in solitude and anxiety, yet enduring all with patience and resignation, and even joy, because she had surrendered her best feelings and sacrificed her own private interests to the advancement of civilization and the great interests of Christianity."

Sweetest of all in her ears were the words spoken about her by David in one of his farewell speeches before leaving England again in March, 1858: "My wife, who has always been the main spoke in my wheel," he said, "will accompany me in this expedition, and will be most useful to me. She is familiar with the languages of South Africa. She is able to work. She is willing to endure, and she well knows that in that country one must put one's hand to everything. . . ."

Mary was thrilled by the thought that she was to go to Africa again to help her husband in his great work. But

Robert, Agnes, and Thomas would have to be left behind, for both parents feared strongly the contamination of heathen Africa for growing young minds and spirits. Mary scarcely knew how she could bear to part from them. Six-year-old Oswell was her comfort when he sailed with her and David from Liverpool on Her Majesty's colonial steamer *Pearl*. On board also were the members of the expedition, under David's leadership, that was to explore the Zambezi and its tributaries.

When they reached the Cape, Mary and David had to part once more, to their bitter disappointment. She was again pregnant and was suffering severely from fever. Her father, who met them at the Cape, took her back with him to Kuruman, in the hope that she would be able to join David on the Zambezi the following year. "It is a great trial to me," Livingstone wrote in his Journal, "for had she come on with us she might have proved of essential service to the expedition in cases of sickness or otherwise, but it may all turn out for the best." Characteristically, he said nothing of his personal disappointment in being deprived of her companionship.

In November of that year Anna Mary was born at Kuruman, a fine, healthy child, but her father, exploring darkest Africa, did not hear of her arrival until a year later. Poor Mary was as much cut off from her husband at Kuruman as she had been in England! If she could not be with him, she would return to their children, Robert, Agnes, and Thomas, in Scotland. But the time she spent in her husband's homeland was unhappy, in spite of the kindness of many friends. Her longing to be with David was intense; her faith in God's loving care tended to founder when she was alone and weighed down by fear that she might never see him again. Bitter slander, utterly without foundation, reached her horrified ears. Her married life, said the gossips, had been unhappy. A doctor of divinity had been heard to say, when her devotion to her family was praised, "Oh, she is no good; she is here because her husband cannot live with her." Even more difficult to bear, and equally false, was the tacit assumption, sometimes stated as actual fact, that David had followed the example of many white men in the tropics in having illicit relationships with African women. In after years Livingstone reproached himself for allowing his anger at this malicious gossip to affect his better judgment: he agreed that Mary should join him at the mouth of the Zambezi, although he knew that it would be better for her to wait until he had founded a settlement on the healthy shores of Lake Nyasa.

It was the last day of January, 1862; signals fluttered from the masthead of H.M.S. *Gorgon,* fresh from England. David strained his eyes and read "Wife aboard." He signaled back from his own ship, the *Pioneer,* "Accept my best thanks"; thus concluding "the most interesting conversation I had engaged in for many a long day." Soon husband and wife were reunited after an absence of nearly four years, during which each, in different ways, had suffered almost to the limit of human endurance.

Within three months they were called upon to face a longer separation, for on April 27, 1862, Mary died. She was unable to resist the fever-laden air of the swamps at the river mouth, and the *Pioneer* was unable to travel up-river to healthier country because the water was too low to enable her to get over the sandbanks.

During those three last months David and Mary were very happy together, planning how she could best help and comfort him during the next stage of their joint work, looking through the boxes of goods she had prepared with loving care and the forethought born of experience. His Puritan conscience feeling almost afraid of such happiness, David said to her, half in earnest and half in fun, "We old bodies ought now to be more sober and not play too much."

"Oh, no, David," she answered quickly, "you must always be playful as you have always been; I would not like you to be as grave as some folks I have seen."

"O my Mary, my Mary," David wrote in the Journal into which he poured his love and heartbreak, "how often we have longed for a quiet home since you and I were cast adrift at Kolobeng. . . . She purposed to do more for me than ever. The loss of my dear Mary lies like a heavy weight on my heart. . . . For the first time in my life I feel willing to die."

Exactly fifty-five years after the death of Livingstone, at which time Christianity had scarcely begun to penetrate the great continent, full-blooded Africans, including two bishops and one woman, were sent by their churches as delegates to the International Missionary Council's meeting at Madras in December, 1938. At that time the total African Christian community, Protestant and Roman Catholic, numbered six and a half million. The Protestant church increased six-fold during the first forty years of this century.

To David Livingstone, more than to any other person, this amazing result is due—to his complete dedication to God's will, to his unflinching singleness of purpose. Jesus said, "He that loveth father or mother more than me is not worthy of me; and he that loveth son or daughter more than me is not worthy of me; and he that doth not take his cross and follow after me, is not worthy of me." David Livingstone did not allow even his love for wife and children to divert him from the lonely course to which God had called him. And Mary, his wife, was not the victim of his selfishness, as some of her partisans hotly declared, but the partner of his enterprise, as much during the periods of separation when her part was confined to waiting and praying as when she was by his side, cheering him with her counsel, her companionship, and her practical help.

Christina Coillard

HOMEMAKER IN THE WAGON

One cold Sunday morning after church fifteen-year-old Christina Mackintosh hurried her younger sister off to the Canongate in Edinburgh, haunt of every kind of misery and wickedness, and left her on a dark landing in a horrible "close." Emerging from a garret, she commanded her frightened sister to take off a new, warm garment that she was wearing, saying, "I've given them mine already." A glimpse of a ragged family in a squalid room, as Christina whisked in and out, and the two girls ran down the stairs and walked shivering homeward. Most parents in 1844 would have forbidden their young daughters to brave what were then the very real dangers of the slums, but their father and mother, a Baptist minister and his wife, had passed on to their children an austere yet warmhearted conception of duty.

Robert Moffat visited Edinburgh about this time, accompanied by Sarah Robey, the African girl whom he and Mary had rescued, as a baby, from being buried alive. When Christina heard him speak, "I will be a missionary and go to Africa," she vowed.

Christina's brothers and sisters dubbed her "the heroine," while her father, with a lively recollection of the tempestuous night in 1829 on which she entered the world, was fond of remarking, "Christina was born in a storm and will live in a storm." The years passed, but no way opened for Christina to go to Africa. The life of a teacher, "wrestling with demons in the shape of boys," as she put it, seemed a tame life for a heroine. In the summer of 1857, however, when she was twenty-eight, she joined her eldest sister in Paris, where Kate was in charge of a Christian residential home for British governesses. An old court lady, whom she met at a friend's house, was delighted with "this *fraîche* Christina, pretty, but somewhat indifferent to dress. . . . Witty and full of life, in her manner to me respect always mingled with a charm which makes one forget one is old."

A few days after her arrival in Paris, Christina was taken to hear François Coillard. Nearly five years younger than herself, but looking older, with his serious face framed in side whiskers above a high collar, this peasant descendant of Huguenot martyrs was under orders for Africa. When Christina was introduced to him a few days later by Madame André-Walther, whose home was a rallying center for French Evangelicals, he fell instantly in love with the graceful, lively Scots girl, her rosy face and sparkling eyes shaded by a large straw hat. "I knew that she only could complete my life," he wrote. But his time was short, and he was harassed by many

scruples. Ought a missionary to marry? Was his love a temptation of the Evil One to hinder him in his work?

In his perplexity Coillard consulted Madame André. She,
kind woman, suggested that he and a friend should escort
Christina and her sister to see the sights on the fifteenth of
August, when Paris was illuminated in honor of the emperor. "I scarcely remember the illuminations," Coillard
wrote, "for other thoughts preoccupied my heart. I said little;
she said little; for I did not know English then, and she, just
arrived from Scotland, knew little French. We understood
each other for all that, and she gave many proofs of her devotion and her affection for missions." From the beginning,
Christina had a premonition that François was her destined
husband, but, as he realized, her devotion was given at first to
the missionary rather than to the man. Within a month he
sailed for Africa, without coming to a decision.

When at length he wrote from Africa to ask her to marry
him, her family and friends, all except her sister Kate, implored her "not to bury herself and her talents in Africa."
The opposition was so strong that she yielded to it, probably
the only time in her life when she allowed others to decide for
her. She replied to François that she did not know him well
enough to marry him. After two years he wrote again, and
this time she accepted him. The early call to Africa had been
repeated and again she responded; but this time she realized
the cost as the impetuous girl of fifteen had not. She must
obey; but she was without joy in the prospect of giving her
life to Africa, "the grave of all her ambitions and of all her
tastes." François' letters are full of sympathy and gratitude.
"I do not know," he wrote, "that I could do what you are
doing, giving up all for an unknown country and an almost

unknown husband. . . . May I, by my constant love, fill all the empty places of your heart." She sailed for South Africa in November, 1860. Her anguish was so terrible at leaving her family and friends, and the rich intellectual and social life that she loved, that forty-five years later her sister was to write, "Such grief I never saw and can hardly bear to think of now."

She landed at Cape Town, and François, owing to a misunderstanding, had gone to meet her at Port Elizabeth, five hundred miles away. His chivalrous soul sick with disappointment, he could not wait to go round by boat but set off by post cart, traveling night and day over rough roads and along narrow ledges through the mountains. When the story of his breakneck drive reached Paris, the director of missions thought it his duty to send the eager young bridegroom an official rebuke for risking his valuable life in this totally unnecessary fashion; but he added an unofficial postscript to tell him that he liked it all the same, and was glad of this proof that chivalry was not yet dead among the sons of France!

The wedding of Christina and François in Cape Town, in February, 1861, was the beginning of an unbroken idyll of married love that lasted for thirty years.

Christina discovered that the Africans, with their happy knack of the appropriate phrase, had nicknamed her husband "father of neatness." To her unspeakable delight, his passionate resolve to keep order and dignity in their lives was scarcely less than her own. To both of them scrupulous attention to cleanliness and neatness in their dress and surroundings, to courtesy and grace in daily living, were everyday requirements, not optional extras for the fastidious. If the missionary were not himself an example of the graciousness of Christian life, from whom would his converts learn it? So, even when their only home was a traveling wagon in a waterless desert, Christina always managed to have the table laid properly for a meal once a day at least, and husband and wife paid each other the compliment of freshening up their appearance before sitting down to it.

During the first months in Africa, François had believed that his fastidiousness was a temptation to indulgence in comfort and that he must overcome it. But one day, he told Christina, he met a missionary colleague in his wagon returning from six months' travel across an uninhabited desert. When the wagon, torn and battered, jolted to a standstill, the door opened and eight or nine children tumbled out, barefoot, ragged, shockheaded, none too clean. "I was horrified," he said—and Christina's face showed that she fully shared his horror. "I made up my mind then and there that I would never let myself go like that, either in my person or surroundings, however hard it might be to keep up to even the simplest standard of decent living."

"You are right, dear Frank," she responded warmly. "If we want to raise the Africans, we must start from a very high standard and never allow ourselves to sink to their level. For myself," she added with her gay laugh, "I believe I should be unhappy in eternity if the Lord suddenly summoned me home and I had left the house untidy."

Writing to his sister-in-law in Scotland, François cannot lavish enough praise on Christina's taste in decorating the wagon, "so fresh and *mignon*," and he enumerates pretty curtains, leopard-skin rugs, elegant little fittings, and even growing plants.

The first five years of their married life Christina and

François spent at Leribé, in Basutoland, at that time outside the control of any Western government. Coillard happily describes his old station as the "ex-Hermitage." Here he had spent three years of utter loneliness, without a single Christian in the whole district with whom to hold fellowship, "hearing nothing from morning till night and often all night through but the wild shouts, the din of their heathen dances, their drunken brawls." This was the setting into which Christina, sociable, civilized in the best sense, and abhorring domestic drudgery, was transplanted. No wonder that after some months she fell really ill from homesickness. Evening after evening, the day's distasteful work faithfully accomplished, she sat down with a pile of old diaries and her letters and other mementoes of home. She made no complaint, but tears ran silently down the cheeks that, alas, were no longer rosy. François, sensitive and self-distrustful, suffered agonies because of the misery that his love had brought to his radiant Christina.

One day, with characteristic good sense and determination, she decided that she must brood no more. With a firm hand she set fire to all her letters and journals, and resolutely put behind her everything that could draw her thoughts back to the life she had left behind. When François returned, she met him at the door with something of her old sparkle and the exclamation, "I have burned them all. You shall not see me fretting any more. 'Forget thine own people and thy father's house.' "

Christina's life left her little time for moping. She still "wrestled with demons in the shape of boys"—and girls, too, although she could command their attendance at school only when the chief allowed them to come. This chief, Molapo, had at one time come almost to the threshold of the Christian church, and after his rejection of the Truth he alternated between friendship and fierce hostility to the missionaries. At times he feared that under Christina's influence the children were being led to Christianity; then he withdrew his own children from the school and his people were quick to follow suit.

To keep her husband and herself alive and well took up much of Christina's time. The chief's opposition meant that often they could get no help in the house or garden. Every drop of water had to be drawn and carried; firewood must be cut and sometimes brought a long distance; Christina made candles, and spent many hours not only in mending but in making clothes for François as well as for herself. She had no sewing machine until many years later, and their clothes wore out very quickly in the rough life they led. She visited the village women and prescribed medicines and nursed the sick, for she had had much experience of this work in the slums of Edinburgh and Paris. Her cooking was simple enough, because there was so little to cook: "We have no milk because we have no cows; no vegetables nor fruits, because we have no garden, nor meat, because we have no herd; and there is no butcher's shop here"—and, of course, no tinned foods. Whenever they were long enough in one place they planted a vegetable garden, but were often obliged, by lack of water or by opposition, to move to another site before they could harvest its fruits. Their home was first a cottage, then a one-room turf hut, then the wagon for two years. Finally, François built a three-room brick cottage, in which, Christina wrote, "I shall feel like a princess. We feel so the want of having a place where we can shut the door and be quiet."

To their lasting sorrow, they had no children; but they often said that this circumstance meant that they felt hardships and the lack of a settled home less than others might have done. They gratified their love of children by adopting African boys and girls, who thus had the advantage of growing up in a Christian atmosphere, so different from that of brawling drunkenness, which was at times their inevitable environment in a pagan African village.

They reserved two evenings a week for study and reading, and Christina's joy in "abstruse" books provided some of the pleasant fun that is the cement of family life. François loved to tease his wife about her taste for metaphysics. One of his notes to her reads, "I really think we have killed the blue-stocking mouse. She was frisking about this evening in the fresh air, philosophizing, no doubt, about the properties of matter, when we pursued and overtook her, the rogue! She had nibbled plenty out of your books. . . . Poor creature, she was charming, but a thirst for knowledge was her ruin."

In 1865 the existence of the mission, and, at times, the lives of the missionaries, were threatened by devastating war, in which Basutos, the Boers of the Orange Free State, and the British of Natal all played their part. Boundary disputes, cattle raiding, and other depredations by a half-brother of Molapo, which involved the whole Basuto nation, shocking reprisals on the part of the Boers, an astounding defeat of the Boers by the Basutos, and long-continued guerilla warfare made up the shifting pattern of the conflict. The whole country was in arms, and whites and blacks alike shot at sight without regard to age or sex. The mission station at Leribé was transformed into "a perfect Bethesda. People bring us the old, the blind, the infirm, the sick, most of them without food,"

François wrote. "The number of the famine-stricken is increasing every day, and these poor creatures look to us as their providence. It is terrible to have to tell people who are dying of hunger that one has nothing."

With a heavy heart Christina watched François ride off one day in December, 1865, for the mission station at Berea. Knowing that he was liable to be shot at by either side in the war, he carried a white handkerchief tied to a long pole as a flag of truce. Two days later a messenger reached Christina to say that he was dangerously ill and begging her to come at once on horseback; she might be too late if she traveled by wagon. Without waiting even to change her dress for a riding habit, Christina saddled her horse herself and started off with a guide. No fear of warlike bands could keep her from François' side. For sixty miles she rode with the awful fear tugging at her heart that her beloved was already dead. Night fell, and the guide lost his way. In the darkness they wandered among the ravines for more than three hours without striking the trail. At length Christina unsaddled the horse, which could travel no farther, and threw herself on the ground, "pouring out her sorrow unrestrainedly before God, her only Protector." When she reached Berea at two o'clock the next day, she found François slightly improved, but within a few days pleurisy developed and he was again on the very threshold of eternity. Everyone gave up hope but Christina, and she upheld him by her own passionate belief that God did not mean him to die before his work was done.

Late in January, François, though still weak, set out with Christina for Leribé. The village where they spent the night, sharing in a Communion Service with some Basuto Christians from many miles around, was surrounded by Boers, who made a sudden attack at dawn. Faint and ill as he was, François struggled out to the commandant "through a perfect storm of bullets; the ground was covered with the dead and dying." He implored him not to kill the unarmed Christians; "they have come to a church festival; it is like slaughtering sheep." The commandant would do no more than give Coillard a safe conduct for his own three Basuto servants, but without much expectation that it would protect them from being shot at sight. Christina and François reached home with them safely after a terrible journey by night, through villages reduced to ashes, with dogs howling amid the ruins, the awful laughter of hyenas and jackals guiding them past scenes of recent slaughter.

Less than two months later, in March, 1866, orders came from the Boer government of the Orange Free State that the Coillards were to leave Basutoland within two weeks. Before the two weeks had expired, armed men brought wagons to the mission station and carried the missionaries off in such haste that Christina left bread in the oven! "Bidding farewell to our weeping flock, we set off, exiles from our only home on earth." Several Christian Basutos went into exile with them, including two small boys, their adopted children. After an exhausting and perilous journey, they reached Natal, worn out in body and mind.

Several other missionary families had been exiled from Basutoland with the Coillards, and none of them saw the least hope of being able to return to their work there. Some of them were in correspondence with the missionary head-quarters about work among the French-speaking people of Mauritius, and François was offered a pastorate on that island. Without comment, he told Christina about it, asking her to think it over. They were both broken in health and might have taken an honorable discharge from more pioneer work; the stipend offered, though modest enough, was much larger than they could hope for in Africa, and they had undertaken the education of five of François' nephews and nieces, as well as the support of his mother. But Christina wanted no time to think over the offer, attractive as it might have seemed to some. Instantly she replied, "When God sent us to the heathen in Africa it was for our lifetime, and he will find a way to send us back, if not to the Basutos, to others. And besides, we have really taken a vow of poverty; we must be true to it." Perhaps Coillard had never loved her so well as at that moment. "Thank God," he said, with a sigh of pure relief, "we are of the same mind, and since that is so, we will never discuss it again."

In January, 1868, the British government acceded to the urgent appeal of Moshesh, father of Molapo and overlord of all the Basutos, to take over the government of Basutoland. But Molapo's territory, including Leribé, remained for a time within Boer jurisdiction, and did not come under British protection until April, 1870. In July, 1868, the Coillards risked a visit to their old station, as they were to pass near it during a two-and-a-half-month wagon trek into the Kalahari desert. They found the home of which they had been so proud indescribably dirty, the walls shining with grease and ochre from contact with the bodies of Molapo and his wives, who had been living there. Molapo received them sullenly. He had their former bedroom cleared out; but during their stay they slept on the ground, having "not even the ghost of a mattress."

Molapo left them, and for four days they had a wonderful

time. The Basutoland missionaries had builded better than they knew; and through war and famine and their forced withdrawal from the work, the Holy Spirit worked a great change in the hearts of the people who had before been indolent, indifferent, or antagonistic. From early morning the Coillards were besieged by old and new Christians. François baptized six converts, administered Holy Communion to forty church members, preached to large congregations, and talked with small groups and individuals. "We did not feel tired," is the entry in his Journal, "but profoundly edified and happy. The work of God is greater and more beautiful than we had thought."

In the record of this trek we read of hardships that must have tried their enfeebled bodies almost beyond endurance: "Poor Christina half dead with cold and fatigue." . . . "Marched till sunset without finding water; all set to work to look for it. I returned exhausted." . . . "Towards midnight were awakened by the howling of leopards, who were roaming round the wagon the whole night, and kept us in a continual state of alarm."

At the beginning of 1869 they returned to Leribé, their continued stay being winked at, though not officially sanctioned until the British took over the following year. The journey, during which they visited four distant outstations and crossed the foodless and waterless Kalahari, was full of misery. Bad food and water—strips of *biltong* (dried meat) and dough cakes full of weevils made up their diet—brought Christina to death's door with dysentery. "The wagon and tent like ovens and swarming with flies like bees. . . . A wagon makes a poor hospital" is one of the pitiful entries in François' diary at this time. Before Christina had recovered strength,

François himself was laid low with the same painful and dangerous complaint. They arrived in Leribé white and worn, their clothes in rags, their wagon dilapidated, their provisions exhausted.

During the next seven years they worked happily at Leribé and in the surrounding territory with the help of Basuto evangelists, adding members to the church and doing their part to build up the Basutos into a peaceful Christian nation. At Whitsuntide, 1871, they dedicated a beautiful stone church, seating six hundred people. Three hundred communicants joined with them on that first day of worship. They built a new mission house after many delays and disappointments, a charming small building of brick faced with stone, raised on a pretty natural terrace overlooking the garden and the field sloping down to the river. "People say," wrote Christina proudly, "there is not such a pretty, well-finished house in Basutoland as ours. I think so too." Both were passionately fond of their home and looked forward to spending the remainder of their lives in Leribé, in all the glory of the growing work.

They were planning to return to France for a short holiday in 1875. By that time François would have been in Africa for eighteen years, Christina for fifteen. The climate, the toil, the disappointments, the solitude, had taken serious toll of health and nerves and spirit. They were longing for a fresh revival of power.

But 1875 passed, then 1876. They were still in Africa. In 1877, when Christina was forty-eight, they set out on a missionary journey that lasted for over two years, during which, like Paul, they encountered perils of rivers, of robbers, of hostile chiefs and peoples, and perils of the desert. Like their great predecessor, too, they knew unremitting labor, hunger and thirst, heat and cold and loneliness, the crushing weight of disappointment, yet with all, the glow of hope and the abiding presence of God. Their object was to find a mission field where the Basutos could work, following a great outburst of evangelistic fervor on the part of these Christians of a day.

When François returned from the synod meeting at which he had been asked to take charge of the expedition, Christina met him "with her usual smiling playfulness." He handed her a letter in which he had tried to put the issue before her calmly; on the one side, their trip to Europe, the preparations all made, their families and friends expecting them, their ill-health, their age, the appalling responsibility of the expedition; on the other, renewed and deepened consecration to their Master's service. Christina read the letter and folded it up without a word, but "her expression changed terribly." They spoke little and slept less for several days. The conflict shook them. A friend who was staying with them, who knew little of the struggle through which they were passing, read the Ninety-First Psalm at family prayers. As he read, "He shall give his angels charge over thee," husband and wife looked at each other. The moment they were alone Christina said, "Well, with such an escort we can go anywhere, even to the Zambezi." Their resolution taken, peace and joy returned to their hearts. Christina wrote to her sister, "I think I was too fond of my home and too proud of it, and this must be the reason why I had to be emptied out from vessel to vessel and shaken up."

Missionaries, traders, magistrates, Christian and heathen Basutos, all assembled to see them off in April, 1877. François felt deeply his responsibility for the twenty-seven African members of the expedition: four evangelists with their wives and children, drivers, and young men to lead and graze the cattle. His fifteen-year-old niece, Elise, accompanied them also, and gave to Christina a daughter's loving care and companionship.

Christina's Scottish niece, Catherine Mackintosh, after reading the journals of this trek, comments that her aunt's figure fills the background, "providing every want, foreseeing every emergency." When all the men were exhausted after dragging the wagons through a dry river bed, it was Christina who produced bottle after bottle of cold tea, which she had made at the last stop where water was available. "Oh," cried the men, crowding round her, "you are our mother; you save our lives." When they lost their way through trackless forests Christina took part in the consultations. "She has a power of judgment worth ten men," writes François admiringly. She cut out garments for the catechists' wives to sew during the tedious days in the wagon; she doctored and nursed their children; she classified plants and wrote copious journals; she bargained with painted savages, armed to the teeth, over the amount of food they should give for beads, or a dog, or a blanket, or a hatchet. The startling slenderness of their resources necessitated rigid economy and constant watchfulness: François had outfitted the entire expedition for an expenditure of two hundred and fifty dollars. In the midst of all her cares Christina made time to carry on Elise's education almost as thoroughly as if they had been in a Parisian schoolroom.

The expedition went unarmed, except for guns and a small case of powder needed to shoot game for food, or to protect themselves against wild beasts. Time and again the experience that they had in August, 1877, was paralleled. On this occasion they were in a long, narrow valley between rocky, wooded hills in the territory of the chief, Masonda. After a rude, unceremonious reception by swarms of savages, armed with axes, knives, bows and arrows, Christina and Coillard were invited to visit the chief's mountain fortress. The guides led Christina and Elise by the hand. François, behind them, suddenly realized that they were heading straight for a round, slippery rock overhanging an abyss. He sprang forward to their rescue. Releasing their intended victims, the warriors leaped down the face of the cliff with the sure footing of mountain goats. Later the travelers learned from another tribe that Chief Masonda had actually instructed his followers to "throw the white man's wife and daughter" over the precipice and Coillard after them, and then to massacre their people. "If you escaped Masonda," their informants reasoned, "it is a miracle. Your Jesus is almighty."

The next day the chief came to the wagon, demanding powder. Coillard refused; his was a mission of peace, and he had no powder to sell or give. The chief foamed at the mouth and went off, shouting abuse. Early next morning the travelers inspanned. Instantly the whole valley was alive with armed men bent on plunder. The chief continued to demand powder, but at length accepted an ox. In the very narrowest place, between two walls of rock, the hindmost wagon stuck. The oxen were unyoked, and Christina and Elise sat quietly down under a tree with their sewing. A young savage rushed from behind the tree and began brandishing an ax a few inches from their heads. Rudely the chief replied to Coillard's entreaties, "If you don't like us near, let these women get out of the way; we won't."

Christina gathered all the women and children into one of the wagons, praying with them and keeping them occupied. The oxen, which had been allowed to graze for several hours in preparation for the test that lay ahead, were brought back, and the drivers began to yoke up. The savages closed in on them, led by the chief, and the Basutos, seizing their guns, ran to defend their families. Christina, seeing her husband in danger, rushed to him with a message of encouragement, then back to her charges in the wagon. After an instant of prayer, Coillard begged the Basutos to lay down their guns.

"Would you shed the blood of those you have come to teach?"

"But men should die like men," they muttered.

"No," he said firmly, "a man should die like a Christian first; like a martyr, if need be."

The men laid down their arms, but they begged him to give the chief their box of powder, "to save our children's lives." He hesitated. It was a difficult choice. But he knew he must refuse.

François ordered the drivers to move. They cried "Trek," but their voices trembled so audibly that the oxen refused to budge. Shouts of triumph burst from the warriors' throats. "The night is falling," they cried. "You are in our power. We will have your blood and everything you possess, and we shall see if your God will deliver you." The triumphant shouts of the warriors defeated their own purpose. The oxen were terrified, made a final struggle, and the wagon at last began to move.

In their prayers that night—for the wagon was church and mission station as well as home, and they held regular services for the whole company when they halted—the missionary band gave thanks for their inexplicable escape from the savages who were so many against their few. To Christina and François the explanation of their deliverance and of many similar occurrences was simple: "The angel of the Lord encampeth round about them that fear him and delivereth them."

On this journey Christina had a severe attack of sunstroke, during which she became unconscious. The confession of this brave, strong woman that she was disappointed to return to consciousness helps us to fathom the depths from which she cries, "I did not till then realize how very unutterly weary I had become. . . . I do beg the Lord to restore my bodily health so that I may honestly and faithfully serve him." This sunstroke caused her to suffer terrible pain in the head for the remainder of her life.

Masonda and all the other chiefs of that part of Africa paid tribute to Lobengula, the king of the dreaded and warlike Matabele, whose permission the missionaries must obtain before they could settle in his country. In November, 1877, Lobengula, furious because the expedition had entered his territories, sent out a hundred and fifty armed warriors to bring Coillard and his party to Bulawayo. The prisoners were made to travel night and day, through forests and flooded rivers, over mountains, marshes, and rock-strewn plains. The heat was so intense that sometimes, although they were nearly dying of thirst, they found the water in the barrels too hot for their lips to touch. In spite of all that Christina could do to encourage and help the wives of the evangelists, the poor women were miserable and full of complaints.

The missionaries' captivity in Bulawayo lasted for three dreary months, during which they felt their lives in peril at every moment. Thievish crowds surrounded the wagons at all hours, watching every movement, making insulting remarks, and never leaving the prisoners alone an instant. How they endured the sights and sounds of torture and cruelty they scarcely knew. At length François and the Basuto evangelists were summoned to the court to receive the king's answer to their petition to establish a Christian mission in his territory. The chiefs who surrounded Lobengula shouted insults at them as soon as they appeared. "We hate to see you! There is the road that leads out of our country. Be gone!" Lobengula's country was closed to Christianity.

After a month of forced marches through a burning wilderness, with six invalids among them, they reached Shoshong in April, 1878. In this capital of the African Christian King Khama they remained for two months to enjoy the hospitable kindness of king and people and await guidance for their next move. While in Bulawayo they had met several people from the region north of the Zambezi. These Barotse and their allied tribes actually spoke the language of Basutoland, which had been imposed on them by an earlier conqueror. But the Barotse allowed no outsider to enter their country with the exception of one white trader, and he remained south of the river; no white man had crossed the Zambezi since David Livingstone had done so. Was this coincidence of language the finger of God pointing them to his chosen mission field for the Basuto church? Khama strongly urged the undertaking, and offered to send a chief with them as guide and ambassador.

The party started off for the Zambezi in June, 1878, leaving behind the African wives and children in charge of two of the catechists, and one of the drivers who was ill. He died before the travelers returned. Christina was carried on a litter that her husband had made for her; Elise rode a donkey; the others went on foot, and the wagons lumbered in their wake. A humble, lonely little band, toiling across the bare desert under the burning sun to break down the walls of the forbidden kingdom of the Barotse and take it by storm for their Master.

Seven weeks after leaving Shoshong they arrived at Leshoma, on the south bank of the Zambezi, and sent messengers to Lewanika, who was at that moment in power in "the land of blood," as one of the Barotse had called his country. While awaiting this powerful king's permission to enter his territory, they went on an excursion to the Victoria Falls; Christina and Elise were probably the first European women to see this majestic sight. Soon after their return to Leshoma all, except Christina and one of the catechists, were laid low with fever. For eight days François hung between life and death, and before he was on his feet again another of the Basuto drivers died. Leshoma was infested with lions, which roared round the camp all night. One daring beast even came inside the stockade and killed a dog tethered to the tent in which Elise was sleeping.

An exhausted Portuguese explorer, Serpa Pinto, staggered into their camp one day. When he saw Christina and Elise seated at their embroidery in the midst of such savage surroundings, he feared for a moment that they were but hallucinations caused by his fevered condition. He actually wept when he sat down with his new friends to a meal, meager enough in itself, but raised to the level of a banquet by a delicate white tablecloth, the neatness of his hosts' threadbare clothes, their exquisite courtesy, and the charm of their con-

versation. Pictures of the wagon—"a marvelous wagon"—
glimpses of their life at festivals and on the Sabbath, which
they kept scrupulously, even records of some of their conversations, are to be found in Serpa Pinto's records of his
travels. During François' absence on a preaching and singing
tour in the surrounding villages, Christina nursed the explorer
through a severe attack of fever, sitting with him all night
during his delirium. The heat was intense. The thermometer
stood at 115° during the day. Meanwhile François was nursing one of the Basuto evangelists, who died just after the
message came from Lewanika that he could not receive the
party then, but that they would be welcome to return to his
country the following year.

During their prolonged wanderings Christina always felt
"so homeless," and on their return to Leribé from this expedition, in August, 1879, she found her home "more lovely
and attractive than ever, especially at this season of spring,
when the garden is all ablaze with peach and almond blos-
som." They did not enjoy it for long, however, as in December
they left for their long-delayed furlough in Europe. But even
then they did not rest, for with the exception of five weeks
spent in Scotland with Christina's family, their two years in
France and Britain were spent in a ceaseless round of meetings, speeches, and committees, during which they endeavored
to arouse interest and gather funds for the new mission on
the Zambezi.

Their "home-coming" to Leribé, in August, 1882, was one
of the saddest times in Christina's life. Then, indeed, she felt
homeless, for in a cruel and disastrous war between the rival
supporters of two of Chief Molapo's sons, the mission com-
pound had become a waste, the village was a heap of ashes,

their cattle, corn, and fruit trees had been pillaged. Far worse to them was the discovery that the congregation was scattered, that many of the leading Christians had been killed and that others had relapsed into paganism. The conflict rose to such heights of savagery that old men were murdered and children mutilated in the Coillards' garden, to which they had fled for safety. Some of the cruelties, Christina tells her sister, "are too dreadful even to write," but she adds sorrowfully that she knows them to be quite true.

Through many months of such experiences François and Christina clung faithfully to their determination to accept Lewanika's invitation to enter Barotseland. The Basutos, in the midst of their civil war, had lost interest in what had started as "their own mission," but in January, 1884, four evangelists and their families were eager to go with the party, which included, besides the Coillards and their niece, a young Swiss missionary who married Elise the following year. The expedition started as soon as another missionary couple arrived to take over the work at Leribé.

Unexpected bad news met them at Leshoma on the south bank of the Zambezi: Lewanika had been ousted from his throne because of his ruthless government and a rival king set up in his stead. For thirteen months they waited there in dreary suspense, their lives and their property never safe for a moment. François offered pieces of cloth to a number of men as payment for building a two-room cottage. He kept strictly to the bargain in his scrupulous way, but all the men complained of being underpaid.

Christina came to the rescue. "Here are some beads," she told them gaily. "Every man who has not made a fuss shall have a few."

"*I* have not grumbled," said one virtuously.

"Nor I."

"Nor I."

It appeared that not one of them had made the smallest complaint, and they went off happily with their beads. That evening Christina and François sat together in the moonlight outside the cottage.

"Why are you so sad, *chérie?*" François asked tenderly.

"Don't mind it, Frank," she whispered unsteadily, "but I have seen so many houses like this one since I have been in Africa, and we have been emptied of them all."

Christina was fifty-five by age and many years older by privation and the withering effect of a tropical climate. She was weary to the very core of her being of camping, of never having any privacy, of wild beasts and wild men, of loathsome insects, of the racking pains of her overdriven, rebellious body, of perpetual striving and making-do, of the fight for even the lowest standard of decency and comfort. Above all, perhaps, of the constant and necessary preoccupation with food and the humiliating process of bargaining over its price. Yet it became a daily reminder to her of the love of the Father "who knoweth ye have need of all these things."

In August, 1885, they crossed the Zambezi, and the following month opened the first mission station on the north bank at Sesheke, an important village. The night after they crossed the river Christina happened to be left alone in the camp for a short time. A number of Barotse women rushed in and, throwing themselves at her feet, implored her to protect them. Their men-folk, they said, were being killed by the king's officers, and they expected to be sacrificed also. But the camp was defenseless, without even a stockade, and the missionaries had no shelter to offer the poor creatures. Before dawn they were all caught and massacred.

The shadow of death hung over Barotseland. A man's life was rated far below that of an ox; women had no rights whatever and were scarcely acknowledged to be human. Witchburnings, massacres, ghastly tortures were everyday occurrences. When Lewanika came back to power, he sent for François, and approved his selection of Sefula for the second mission station, three hundred miles to the north of Sesheke, where Elise and her husband were left in charge of the work. François returned to Sesheke to fetch Christina in December, 1886. Their journey to Sefula together was an altogether delightful experience; they were traveling at last toward a permanent home after ten years of wandering. Christina made the wagon gay with flowers. Lewanika came with an escort of musicians and clowns to greet "our mother"; crowds thronged round to look at the white woman. But clouds soon began to obscure this sunny landscape. Five months later Christina wrote, "O, the quantities of people that have been burnt as witches and wizards since we came here. It is almost a daily occurrence."

Within a few weeks the Coillards opened a school, but only the children of the king and the principal chiefs were allowed to attend. The children had slaves to wait on them—one little twelve-year-old princess had three, one to lean against as a cushion, one to hand her her book or slate, and one to have her back used as a writing-desk. Their persons were so sacred that when a servant accidentally brushed against Lewanika's daughter with a bundle of reeds an executioner put him to death within half an hour. The Coillards found it difficult to make much impression in these circumstances and were not deeply distressed when Lewanika ordered that the school should be closed. One of the king's sons, however, who had attended as a pupil was later baptized.

Famine spread through Barotseland as a result of the wild years of anarchy when the cattle had been killed off and no crops sown. The missionaries were robbed of their cattle one by one; everything that grew in their garden was stolen, and they lived for a time on fish and manioc. They knew that at any moment they might be accused of sorcery, the penalty for which was death. After four years they had not made a single convert outside their own household and were still living in the mud hovel they had put up as a temporary shelter when they arrived in Sefula. Christina's health was completely shattered, and only her indomitable will kept her going at all.

In May, 1891, François was summoned by Lewanika to visit him at his capital. Serious misrepresentations had been made against him in the hope of driving Christianity out of the country, and when Christina said good-by she feared she would never see him again.

"Is it all right?" she called out when she heard his step in the distance.

"Yes, it is all right," he replied. "Not a hair of my head has been touched."

But soon Christina was very ill, and in her delirium she lived again some of the periods of anxiety through which they had passed. "My darling, they are slandering you!" she cried over and over.

In October she rose from her sick bed—"so frail she looked like wax"—to accompany François to the capital at the king's urgent invitation. She spent two or three days with the women of Lewanika's household, looking for opportunities of speaking to them of Christ, in the intervals of cutting out and trying on dresses for them. She gave to the king's chief wife a beautiful piece of dress material that had been sent as a present to herself. She was still the same Christina who had stripped off her own clothing to give to a poor family one snowy day in Edinburgh.

"Is it enough for a dress?" asked the princess.

"Yes."

"Then why haven't you made it up for me?"

"Because I am too weak and ill even to sew for myself."

"Then you can take it back. What are you here for if it is not to make dresses for us?"

The great joy of the Coillards on this visit was the public profession of Christian faith made by Litia, Lewanika's son and heir-apparent. He took this step in face of the violent persecution of the chiefs, who said they would never allow him to reign as a Christian king, and who even menaced his life when this threat failed to move him. His friend, who later became prime minister, wept bitterly during his young master's testimony, because, as he said, he felt himself to be such a sinner.

"A Barotse weeping, and weeping for his sins!" exclaimed Christina. "It is a sight I would have traveled a thousand miles to see."

A few days later she begged François to take her back to Sefula, for "I cannot die here." She lived for ten days, but on October 28, 1891, François was left alone and inconsolable. Christina, who had felt so homeless in Africa, had found her home at the last. "Let us be in earnest, in earnest!" were some of the words she spoke toward the end. "How swiftly they have passed, all those years, how little I have done! Do be in earnest, do!"

"For her all is peace," François said. "But," he added sadly, "for me what a terrible solitude. I shall never now have a home on earth."

During their long years in Africa, Christina and François could truly say, "For we have not here an abiding city, but we seek after the city which is to come."

Mary Williams

FRIEND OF THE ISLAND WOMEN

A lively interest in ladies' bonnets and even detailed descriptions of their style, with other particulars about dress, are unusual "finds" in a missionary's diary and letters. They abound in those of John Williams and of Mary, his wife. In his first letter home from the South Sea island of Eimeo, where the young couple landed on November 17, 1817, exactly a year after they had sailed down the Thames from London, John writes with enthusiasm of attending a Christian service with the islanders: "It was pleasing to see so many fine looking females; dressed in white native cloth, and their heads decorated with white flowers and coco-nut leaves plaited in the shape of the front of a cottage bonnet, surrounding the preacher who occupied the centre of the place."

The twenty-year-old ex-ironmonger's apprentice, without

much formal education or theological training, who married the shy, gentle Sunday school teacher, Mary Chauner, in October, 1816, had a strong sense of order and decorum. His practical genius, aided by Mary's skill, helped the savage natives of many South Sea islands not only to exchange faith in hideous fetishes for the worship of the God and Father of our Lord Jesus Christ, but to build churches and comfortable houses, make furniture, spin and weave, put on clothes instead of paint, grow varied food, and employ themselves in many useful industries instead of lying indolently beneath the breadfruit trees, with intervals of fierce fighting and abominable pagan rites.

Their long voyage by sailing ship was tedious, even when broken by some weeks in Rio de Janeiro—where they were joined by their future co-workers, Mr. and Mrs. Lancelot Threlkeld—Hobart, Sydney, and New Zealand. When at last they descried Tahiti their "hearts leaped for joy at the sight of the long-wished-for land."

Before they had been two months on the neighboring island of Eimeo, where they were busily learning the Tahitian language, their first child, John Chauner, was born. Writing to tell her own mother in faraway England of the baby's birth, Mary pleads for her prayers: "You know what anxious cares these dear little treasures bring with them, cares such as none but parents know. But you are not aware of the temptations to which they are exposed here: wickedness which makes our hearts shrink and tremble. We earnestly entreat your prayers, that we may have guidance and grace to train up our little one in the fear of the Lord."

When little Johnny was nine months old, his parents, with Mr. and Mrs. Threlkeld, left the comparative safety and comfort of Eimeo to settle on the island of Raiatea, the largest and most central of the Society Islands, about one hundred miles from Tahiti. As they approached the noble reef that guards the island, Mary was awed by the frowning majesty of the huge mountain masses rising abruptly above the level of the sea. But when they had sailed through an opening in the reef into the placid lagoon, she exclaimed with wonder at the radiant beauty of the scene that lay before her. Rainbow-hued fish darted among forests of coral, making a marine fairyland; crystal streams leaped over the dark rocks and rushed down to water the fertile valleys, covering them with dense vegetation.

But the islanders gave them little time for admiring scenery. "As soon as we landed," John wrote home, "they made a feast for us, consisting of five large hogs for myself, five for Mrs. Williams, and one for our little Johnny. The same provision was made for Mr. Threlkeld." A lavish welcome indeed!

Although about two years earlier the Raiateans had made a profession of Christianity, adopting it as the national religion, their customs were still, the missionaries wrote, "abominable." Raiatea had been the center of a system of idolatry widespread among the surrounding islands; its kings and chiefs had been worshiped as divine; there countless human sacrifices had been offered on the open-air stone altar of Oro. But although still amoral and indolent, the islanders no longer practised human sacrifice and ritual infanticide. Mary discovered with horror that one of her household servants had previously plied infanticide as her trade. She described to her shuddering mistress the various methods she had used, from simple strangulation to burial alive and a lingering death by breaking the infant's joints. On one occasion Mary found herself quietly sewing with three island women, "motherly and respectable," who had among them destroyed twenty-one of their own children.

One of John's first duties was to build a house for his family, "for the missionary does not go to barbarize himself but to elevate the heathen: not to sink himself to their standard, but to raise them to his." Never did wife start house-keeping with greater pride than Mary, when she moved into a seven-room house, built almost entirely by her husband's labor, with a veranda and venetian blinds, the walls plastered with whitewash colored with powdered coral. The furniture, too, was all John's work; and tables, chairs, sofas, and bedsteads caused the wondering islanders to admire and envy. Flower garden, kitchen garden, and poultry yard completed the mission premises. Writing home about her housekeeping, she wishes her mother could taste breadfruit and some of her arrowroot cakes. "I daresay you frequently talk of us," she goes on, "and wonder what we have to eat. There are plenty of fowls here and we dress them in a variety of ways. Sometimes we have fresh pork, and occasionally we kill a suckling pig and get it cooked as well as you can in England, who have large kitchen fires. I only wish we had a cow and then I should be able to make butter, but we get plenty of milk for our tea, as we have five goats." John adds a heartfelt remark to this domestic chronicle: "My dear Mary is a famous cook; I am sure I don't know what a poor man would do by himself in such a place as this."

So many of the island people came to the classes that were taught by Mary and John and the Threlkelds that it was exceptional to see a man or a woman sitting at home during school hours—6 to 8 A.M. Old men, and young women with infants in their arms, ancient grannies, boys and girls of all ages, and the once cruel priests of Oro whose hands had often been stained with the blood of human sacrifice, sat together on the same forms, learning the difference between A, B, and C. Some of them were never able to get beyond "the B A ba," as one discouraged old man lamented; but many of them, including the king and queen, were soon able to read the Gospel of Luke in their own language, translated for them by John, printed on a hand press, and folded and bound by the islanders themselves. Later the children and the adults were taught separately.

The whole island was stirred by the sight of some hundreds of children walking in procession to a feast, provided by the missionaries, to be followed by a public examination in Scripture knowledge for the benefit of their wondering elders. Mary held Johnny more closely as she read one of the banners that the girls and boys themselves had prepared: "Had it not been for the gospel we should have been destroyed as soon as we were born," and saw the troubled faces of those older parents whose children had all been killed in infancy. One aged chief could not contain his grief. In a trembling voice he cried out, "Oh that I had known that the gospel was coming; then I should have saved my children. Alas, I destroyed them all; I have not one left although I have been the father of nineteen children." Being of a very high rank, this chief had had to sacrifice them all in accordance with the pagan laws; other men, according to their position in the tribe, were allowed to keep subsequent children after they had destroyed two, or four, or six. Mothers, however, had often voluntarily sacrificed their children because in the sudden and desolating wars that decimated the islands the care of a family was an added source of horror and distress.

One evening, in June, 1820, as Mary and John sat at dinner, they heard a commotion outside. Through the window they saw a man dancing in front of their house, brandishing a carving knife and shouting, "Turn out the hog, let us kill him! Turn out the pig, let us cut his throat!" Although annoyed at the disturbance, John could scarcely keep from smiling at the man's odd appearance, for he was wearing a pair of trousers as a jacket, and a red shirt instead of trousers. He rose from the table to speak to the man from the doorway and ask him to go away. Before he could reach the door, however, one of the Raiatean deacons of the church burst into the house, almost breathless with running, and cried, "Why do you expose your life? *You* are the pig he is calling for; you will be dead in a moment." A few of the wilder spirits among the young men, resenting the restraints imposed by Christianity, had tried on two successive days to murder the unsuspecting John. Their first plan was foiled because, having freshly painted his canoe, he failed to oblige them by going out in it to be thrown overboard as they had intended; the second time he was saved because one of the conspirators repented of his share in the business and divulged the details of the murderous plot in time for John to receive the deacon's warning.

Poor, trembling Mary clung to the husband who had been so miraculously preserved to her, but all her joy and thankfulness could not save her from the effect of shock. Her second child was prematurely born and died within a few days, while for many anxious weeks John feared that he would lose Mary, too.

Writing home in 1825, John makes one of his many references to Mary's ill-health. She suffered severely from the enervating tropical climate, with its extreme heat, violent hurricanes, and storms. Seven of their children were either born prematurely or died in infancy. Yet, "in every other respect we enjoy a greater share of happiness than usually falls to the lot of man. We are happy in each other, happy in our work, and, with trifling exceptions, happy in the people among whom we labor."

Mary's tender heart was sad for the old women whom she saw huddled in their huts, dirty and uncared-for and unwanted. Before Christianity came to Raiatea, she knew that they would have been killed by their children or friends as soon as they became a burden, but although, as Christians, the islanders spared their lives, they did nothing to make them happy. So she asked a few of the younger women in the church to help her to gather these poor old people into classes, which were held twice a week.

Her first care was to make them decent clothes. She cut out dresses, which her native helpers put together. She fashioned bonnets for them out of native bark cloth and coconut fiber and trimmed them with grasses and shells. As soon as the clothes were ready she invited the old people to a feast. The blind, the lame, the deaf, the decrepit—all were there, some seventy or eighty of them. "We were despised and neglected," said one; "now we are sought out by our elder sister and eat what our ancestors never saw or heard of—English food." (Mary gave them rice and treacle.) "We were dirty and ragged," said another; "now we have good cloth and even coverings for our heads." One guest with a radiant face rose to thank Mary: "It is good we lived to see these days.

We were laid aside as castaways, but now we are beginning to live again. To the word and compassion of God are we indebted."

These old women sat together in front of the pulpit and were among the most attentive in John's congregation. Every Monday afternoon Mary discussed the previous day's sermon with them, and they prayed together. How delighted Mary was when they agreed among themselves to work together on two large mats—one of their few native handicrafts—for her home! Years later, in a far-distant island, John found a similar class for unwanted old people. It had been started by a Raiatean teacher's wife, who had been one of Mary's chief helpers and who had caught from her white friend the warmth and tenderness of Christian compassion for the helpless and despised.

Mary met with another class twice a week—about twenty islanders who seemed most deeply devoted to their new Master. She scorned her ill-health, was even resigned to the loss of her babies, as she looked round the circle of brown faces, alight with intelligence, awed by the wonder of the love of God, and heard the new disciples read in their own language a chapter from one of the Gospels, which her husband had translated. How richly worth while it was! In her heart she thanked God for the great privilege of being a missionary. In after years, many of the women in that class became missionaries in their turn, accompanying their husbands as teachers to other islands where the people still lived in darkness and in the shadow of death.

One evening, as they sat in their comfortable living room, Mary studied her husband with wifely penetration. At length she asked gently: "What is troubling you, John? You have been pretending to read this last hour but you have not turned a single page. And you have been restless and anxious for weeks past, haven't you?"

"Yes, dear"—and Mary smiled as he began to stride about the room in his usual energetic way. "You see, I am not doing enough work. I am sure Jesus doesn't intend a missionary to be contented with a congregation of a few hundred natives, while thousands around him are eating each other's flesh and drinking each other's blood with savage delight, living and dying without knowledge of the gospel." Suddenly he stopped in front of her, his voice vibrant with emotion. "It is our duty, I am convinced of it, Mary, to visit the surrounding islands. I, for my part, cannot content myself within the limits of a single reef."

So began for Mary those years of separation and loneliness, of racking anxiety and fear, which she endured as a good soldier of Jesus Christ. Her husband sailed over a hundred thousand miles to establish missions in the different groups of islands that dot the Pacific Ocean like "clusters of daisies in a stupendous meadow," taking native Christian teachers and their wives to carry on the work that he began. Mary accompanied him on some of the voyages, although she suffered terribly from seasickness in the small, pitching sailing craft when the ocean was at all rough. Four-year-old Johnny was the first white child ever seen by the islanders of Rurutu, who rubbed noses with him and expressed their sorrow that "so young and lovely a child" should be exposed to the dangers of the "wide-spreading boisterous ocean." They begged his parents to give the child to them, saying that they would make him their king. After John had politely declined this flattering offer, the islanders became so insistent that Mary, who suspected them of cannibal tendencies, hurried Johnny away to the cabin.

Whether she voyaged with John or stayed without any white companionship on her island home—for the Threlkelds were soon sent elsewhere—Mary's life was full of tension. In her husband's absence she was often called upon to make quick decisions, sometimes affecting many lives. While John and Chief Tamatoa and many of the older men were away from the island, a ship commanded by an ex-convict sailed into the harbor. The following day Mary was quietly working when two women burst into the room. "Oh, come quickly, please, Mrs. Williams. Many of our men will be killed if you do not come quickly."

As she hurried with them to the beach, Mary tried to make out the cause of the trouble. The ex-convict captain had cheated other islands of their harbor dues, the women explained. A fiery young Raiatean chieftain had gone aboard to demand the money, and the captain had immediately pointed a loaded pistol at his head. "He came ashore," the women panted, "but now he has collected a large party of our men and they have gone aboard the ship, all armed, to have their revenge."

Mary found hundreds of islanders on the beach, shouting and gesticulating. They were in an ugly temper, but they obeyed her sullenly when she forbade any more going off to the ship. Finding some men whom she could trust, she instantly sent them off in a canoe with a note to the captain begging him to pay the small sum due. "And tell our men on board," she said, "that they must come back at once. Beg them from me not to offer any violence to the captain or to take any goods out of the ship."

Anxiously she gazed toward the vessel. Would she be in time? Would the men bow to the authority of a woman, even though she was the missionary's wife? The strain was terrible, until at last she saw black bodies dropping over the sides into the canoes, which were swiftly paddled ashore. Her prompt action had averted a terrible tragedy, for the islanders had already begun to dismantle the ship, while the captain stood with loaded pistols ready to fire into a barrel of gunpowder to blow up the vessel and all on board.

After he had made contacts with the islands in the Hervey group and left devoted Christian islanders from Raiatea to carry on the work, John began to long to take a voyage westward to the distant Navigator (Samoan) Islands and the New Hebrides.

"And how far away are these islands, John, and how long would you be gone?" his wife asked when he began unfolding his plans.

"About eighteen hundred to two thousand miles, my dear, and I should be away about six months, if all went well. You would wish me Godspeed, Mary? If only I had a ship at my command, every island in the Pacific should hear the gospel."

But Mary scarcely heard him to the end before exclaiming with a vehemence so unlike her usual manner that he was completely taken aback: "How can you expect, John, that I should give my consent to such a strange proposal? You will be eighteen hundred miles away, and six months absent, and you will be going among the most savage people we have yet heard about. If all goes well, you say! If you should lose your life in the attempt I should be left a widow with my fatherless children, twenty thousand miles from my friends and my home. Indeed I cannot consent to your going. You must not expect it of me."

Faced by this unexpected resistance, John could say no more. He acknowledged the justice of Mary's plea, but his heart did not relinquish its daring project. "His ardent soul winged its way from island to island," wrote one of his missionary colleagues. "It was vain to raise objections. The thing was so clear to his own mind that he could not for a moment doubt its practicability." Sometimes Mary felt like a dove mated with an eagle.

Rarotonga, which Mary visited with her husband in 1827, he himself having discovered the island on an earlier voyage, had no proper harbor, so that they had to drop into a small boat about three miles from shore. With Johnny and small Sam to look after, the transfer was anything but easy. The wind was very boisterous, the sea exceedingly rough, and the boat old and leaky. Crouched on the floor boards in several inches of water, Mary was obliged to keep on bailing for their very lives. When they landed, they received the congratulations of "the greatest concourse of people I had seen since we left England" on their escape from the very considerable danger of the hazardous passage.

Although they had intended a visit of only four months or so to Rarotonga, they remained for a year. The hospitable natives, who had made bonfires of hundreds of hideous idols only two years earlier, went in procession to convey their guests to the house prepared for them. Everyone was anxious to carry something. One seized a frying pan, another a teakettle, one a bedpost. Somewhat to her confusion, Mary also was picked up by a herculean native and carried on his shoulder over a road slippery with mud after a tropical storm.

Early in their visit Mary was suddenly taken violently ill, and soon became unconscious. Within ten days, however, she had sufficiently recovered to be able to talk. "John," she whispered, "while I have been so ill I have been thinking how I opposed your voyage to the Navigator Islands. I know that you still feel it right to go, and I am thankful that God has permitted me to live to give my full consent. When you go I shall follow you every day with my prayers that God may preserve you from danger, crown your attempt with success, and bring you back in safety."

Well might John's biographer write of Mary, "In Christian heroism she proved the equal of her intrepid husband, and in patient endurance his superior!"

Regarding Mary's unexpected change of opinion as a sign that God wished him to go on with the plan, John actually determined to build a vessel in which to make the longed-for voyage, for no passenger ship sailed the Pacific, and the missionaries were dependent on an occasional man-of-war or trading ship for journeys too long to be risked in native canoes. "Although I knew little of shipbuilding," he wrote, "and had scarcely any tools to work with, I succeeded, in about three months, in completing a vessel of between seventy and eighty tons burden, with no other assistance than that which the natives could render, who were wholly unacquainted with any mechanical art." What amazing ingenuity and persistence!

We can imagine the feelings with which Mary watched her husband and a native crew sail away on their trial trip in *The Messenger of Peace*. Would the clumsy-looking vessel prove seaworthy? Would John be able to navigate her? She was deeply thankful when they returned safely after two weeks or so from an island about one hundred and seventy miles distant with a singular cargo: pigs, cats, and coconuts! Mary hoped that the cats would rid the island of rats. While the household were at family prayers "these disgusting little animals" ran all over them; it was impossible to keep them out of the beds, and at meal times two attendants were occupied in keeping them off the table. As a matter of fact, the "exceedingly voracious" pigs did more than the cats toward ridding Rarotonga of the pests.

In addition to holding daily religious classes for the women while on Rarotonga, Mary made some hundreds of bonnets, and taught many of the island women the art, as well as showing them how to make clothes. She was helped by Mrs. Pitman, a young missionary wife, who had sailed with them to Rarotonga and later settled there with her husband. The native teachers from Raiatea, who had taken the gospel to Rarotonga, were both single men, who, says John with sly amusement, had done their best to teach the women this important branch of knowledge, "but their taste in forming the shape of the bonnets did not admit of equal commendation with their desire to raise the character and promote the comfort of the female sex."

Christianity, as it took root in the islands, brought a tremendous change in the lives of the women. Their husbands no longer tyrannized over them and treated them as inferiors. On every island where John landed the women begged for Christian women to teach them. "Have you not one little bit of compassion for us?" they asked. "Is it only the men who have souls? Do not women require a teacher, too?"

Wherever the Christian teachers' wives went they carried with them not only the knowledge of the gospel that they had caught from Mary but the domestic arts and skills that she had taught them. Their neat clothes were the outward sign of a growth in self-respect and of the dignity conferred on womanhood by Jesus Christ. They presented a striking contrast to the singular appearance of the island women among whom they settled, some of whom were dressed in "a wreath of flowers, a little rouge and oil, a blue bead or two about the neck, and a girdle of fresh-gathered leaves." Many of them were smeared with paint and grease. The styles of hairdressing were exceedingly grotesque, one of the most startling being the head completely shaven, with a single lock of hair dangling to a considerable length from a spot above the left temple. Other island belles had one side of the head shorn, while a rich profusion of curls decorated the other.

On Tonga, where John landed Christian teachers and their wives during his first visit to Samoa, in 1830, he found that the king and queen and some four hundred of their subjects were professing Christians, but until that time they had never been visited by Christian women. The queen was much attracted by the clothing of the Raiatean teachers' wives, made under Mary's guidance. At her special request they made her a bonnet of similar shape and materials, working quickly to have it ready for Sunday. Within a few months all the Christian women of Tonga had been initiated into the mysteries of sewing and other feminine accomplishments. Through the growing self-respect and industry of the women, real family life came to Tonga, as to many other islands, for the first time.

As John watched the young, purchased wives of an "old and unlovely" chief dancing in his honor on an island of the

Samoan group, he prayed that "by the blessing of God upon our labors the day may speedily arrive that these interesting females should be elevated from this terrible degradation, and by the benign influence of Christianity be raised to the dignity of companionship with their husbands and occupy that station in the social and domestic circle which the females of Tahiti, Rarotonga and of other islands have attained since the introduction of the Gospel."

In September, 1831, Mary left Raiatea to revisit Rarotonga, with John and their two sons, Johnny and Sam. Williams wished to consult with Pitman and Buzzacott, the two missionaries there, about the translation of the New Testament into the Rarotonga tongue, on which all three were working, and Mary hoped, by a change of scene, that she might be "spared the distress of consigning a seventh sweet babe to a premature grave."

All went well until the morning of December 21. The Williams' were living with the Pitmans, about eight miles from the Buzzacotts, who had settled near the harbor. A note from Buzzacott warned John that a very heavy sea was rolling in, which, if the wind increased, might drive *The Messenger of Peace* ashore. John set off for the harbor, leaving Mary with the Pitmans. That night the hurricane struck the island with almost unbelievable force.

Mrs. Pitman rushed into Mary's room and urged her out of bed two minutes before a violent gust of wind forced in the end wall of the house. It fell with a crash on the very spot where Mary had been lying. Wrapping themselves in blankets, they all rushed out of the house as the roof began to collapse. Learning that one of the servants' houses was still standing, they were making their way toward it when a coconut tree crashed down on the house, severing it in two. Feeling safer away from houses and trees, they clung together in an open space, exposed to all the fury of the raging elements. The wind howled, the rain came down in deluging torrents, the thunder rolled and pealed, and the lightning darted its fiery flashes among the dense black clouds. Women and children screamed in terror, men shouted, houses crashed to the ground, "the whole island trembled to its very center as the infuriated billows burst upon its shores." Wet through and utterly exhausted, Mary, supported by Mr. and Mrs. Pitman, at length reached the chief's house, which he had made as secure as possible with ropes. There John found her the following day, so ill that he more than once feared that she had ceased to breathe. A few days later yet another still-born infant was "planted" (in the language of five-year-old Sam) in the soil of yet another tropical island.

The hurricane had destroyed nearly a thousand houses on Rarotonga, and all the breadfruit, banana, and coconut trees, on which the people depended so largely for food. The splendid new church and the schoolhouse had been washed away also, while in the harbor *The Messenger of Peace* had been lifted bodily on a tidal wave and carried several hundred yards inland, to come to rest unharmed amid a grove of chestnut trees.

Mary remained on Rarotonga while John sailed first to Tahiti, to fetch food for the nearly-starving islanders, and then again to the Samoan Islands. Among the cargo that he brought back were horses, asses, and cattle. He and Mary had not tasted beef for more than ten years, and they and the missionaries from neighboring islands were eagerly looking forward to a treat when they killed the first ox. Alas, they had so entirely lost their relish for the unaccustomed food that none of them could bear either the taste or smell of it! One missionary wife actually burst into tears, and "lamented bitterly that she should have become so barbarous as to have lost her relish for English beef."

Early in 1833, shortly after John's return from his second voyage to Samoa, he and Mary welcomed their tenth child. Willy was the third who lived and thrived, and they were full of joy at this unexpected blessing after so many disappointed hopes.

In April, 1838, Mary and John once more sailed down the Thames, their faces again toward the South Sea islands, which their hearts had never left, even during three or four years in England.

"How different this voyage is from the one we set out on just twenty-two years ago, John!" said Mary, as they paced the deck of the brig *Camden,* a gift to the South Seas mission from the churches of Britain. "Shouldn't we have been surprised if we could have looked into the future and seen ourselves sailing to the South Seas in a missionary ship and taking out sixteen other missionaries, as well as our own son and his wife?"

"Even six months ago I scarcely expected that *you* would be on board, my dear," he answered, gazing with joy at the beloved companion who seemed to have been given back to him from the grave. For Mary's health had been so cruelly shattered by all her experiences that while in England she had found it impossible to face with equanimity the prospect of a return to the rigors of South Sea island life. John was actually facing the heart-searching choice of leaving her in England or giving up the work that he was sure God meant him to do, when suddenly Mary's health was restored and "she began to anticipate with pleasure what had previously filled her with dismay."

The years in Britain were eventful. John spoke to enthusiastic audiences all over the country, and he published a book, dedicated by permission to King William the Fourth, which introduced Christian work in the South Seas to influential people all over the land. Not even to the king, however, did he present so richly bound a copy as the one that he gave to "my dearest Mary," with the tender inscription: "I present this faithful record of our mutual labours and successes as a testimony of my unabated affection: and I sincerely pray that, if we are spared twenty years longer, the retrospect may afford equal, if not greater, cause for grateful satisfaction."

Toward the end of November the *Camden* anchored in a sheltered harbor in Samoa. Williams had already made up his mind to try to place teachers on some of the Melanesian islands, whose fierce black cannibal inhabitants made the brown Polynesian islanders of Raiatea and Rarotonga seem mild by comparison. He could not take Mary on such a dangerous voyage, so he settled her at Upolu with their son John and his wife and young Willy, in a district where some three or four thousand people were clamoring for Christian teaching.

"And please, please, John, I beg of you not to land on Erromanga. The people there are the most wild and cruel that ever we have heard of. You remember how Captain Cook and his men were very nearly murdered there. And now that all those islanders have suffered so cruelly at the hands of the sandal-wood traders they will hate all white people more fiercely than ever. Please, *please,* dear John, do not land there."

With these reiterated warnings of Mary's ringing in his ears, John said farewell to his wife and family on November 3, 1839, and sailed southwestward into perilous seas in the *Camden.*

Four months later H.M.S. *Favourite* reached Samoa. A heavy-hearted messenger made his way to the house where Mary was living. She was awakened in the middle of the night to hear the news that her fears had many times anticipated: "Mrs. Williams, your husband landed on the beach at Erromanga two weeks after he left you. At first the natives seemed friendly. But suddenly they attacked him from behind and he was clubbed and pierced with arrows as he tried to reach the boat. The captain of the *Camden* was unable to recover his body. You will realize what that means." He paused. Mary shuddered uncontrollably as she whispered, "A cannibal feast?" Her visitor bowed his head sympathetically. After a few moments' silence he went on: "Under the protection of the *Favourite's* guns we managed to land and have brought the skull and other bones for burial here."

For hours Mary remained stunned; she could neither speak nor weep. All around she heard the wailing of chiefs, teachers, and other natives, even those who were not Christians: "Alas, Williamu! Alas, our father!" Toward evening she allowed the chief, Malietoa, to come to her. Kneeling by the sofa on which she lay, he gently took her hand. "O my mother," he said, with tears streaming down his cheeks, "do not grieve so much. You, too, will die with sorrow and be taken away from us, and then what shall we do? Think of John, and of your very little boy who is with you, and think of that other little one in a far distant land, and do not kill yourself."

Day after day the men who had loved Williams came to weep with her, and in sharing their grief she found some assuagement of her own.

Agnes Watt

"NO ORDINARY WOMAN"

Yｏu know, William," said Agnes Watt to her tall, bearded husband of a month, "I went through a very unhappy time after you asked me to marry you. Not that I wasn't already very fond of you, dear," she hastened to add, "and you know I had always felt that God was calling me to be a missionary."

"Which, at any rate at present, means a missionary's wife," her husband interjected, smiling.

"Yes, I realized when you asked me to go with you to the South Seas that God was opening a door into missionary life that might otherwise remain closed to me. But to leave Mother and Father—and our big, happy family party—they felt it so much, too—and perhaps never to see them again— that was why I hesitated"—and her eyes filled with tears as she remembered the nights of anguish and weary questioning that she had endured before she had made William happy by her acceptance.

They were leaning side by side over the rail of the small sailing ship that was carrying them to New Zealand on their way to the New Hebrides.

"I sometimes wonder, Nancy, how I could ever have asked you to make such a sacrifice," he said after a few moments. "And yet I scarcely know how I could face without you all that may lie ahead of loneliness and discouragement. The poor, downtrodden women of the islands, too, need a woman like you to love them into believing that God is a Father who cares as much for them as he does for men."

"I do hope, William, so much, that we may be sent to Tanna. I have the strongest desire to go there, although I know the work is harder than on any of the other islands. To think that it is almost thirty years since John Williams landed three Samoan Christian teachers there the day before he was murdered on Erromanga, and that the Tannese have remained stubbornly heathen ever since! I feel a tremendous urge to carry on the work of those brave men and women who have gone as missionaries through all these years and have either been killed and eaten, or driven away."

"Your parents felt the danger for you, and I cannot wonder," her husband replied in a low voice, remembering the martyrs, white and brown, who had given their lives for the Tannese. "But I know you don't dwell on that side of it."

"No, indeed," said his buxom Scots bride cheerfully. "Now that the parting from my dear ones is over, I am completely happy. What could any woman want more than to go with the husband she loves to do the most worth-while work in the world? We have heard the cry, 'Come over and help us,' and our duty is to obey and leave the future in His unerring hand."

Agnes and William were married in April, 1868, in Glasgow, where Agnes had been born twenty-two years earlier. They sailed immediately for New Zealand to be present at the Assembly of the Presbyterian Church there, which had made itself responsible for their modest salary of seven hundred and fifty dollars a year. Agnes had the wish of her heart fulfilled, for they were asked to open a new station on Tanna. Throughout her twenty-five years of missionary service there, she remained the same loving daughter and sister, writing long letters home and keeping them up to date until a ship called by which she could send them off. These letters give almost a day-by-day record of her experiences, full of vivid detail and wise observation on the Tannese people, their beliefs and ways of life, and their attitude to Christianity.

Captain Cook, who first surveyed Tanna in 1774, formed the lowest opinion of its inhabitants. Not only were they sullen, fickle, and unfriendly, but they were insolent and daring thieves, and practised cannibalism. Missionaries and traders who went to the island in later years had little encouragement to think more highly of them.

Agnes had her first sight of the large mountainous island in April, 1869. It was night when the little mission boat, the *Dayspring,* approached Port Resolution (so-called by Captain Cook after his vessel), and she was struck by the splendor of the very active volcano that blazed up every few minutes. For eight months Port Resolution had been in charge of Thomas Neilson. His wife was a daughter of the Canadian, John Geddie, the pioneer missionary in the New Hebrides, whose success on Aneityum, after many setbacks, was such an inspiration to the workers on Tanna. Christian teachers from

Aneityum, with their wives, were waiting to greet the Watts at Kwamera, where they were to settle. They had already put up a small grass church and a temporary house.

The Tannese were consumed with curiosity about Agnes and her house and furniture, and she wisely realized that she must keep them within bounds or she would have no privacy at all, as she had noticed was the case in some of the missionary households they had visited in their trip among the islands in the *Dayspring*. So she ruled that her bedroom was *i-tapu*—private or sacred; it was to be seen only once by each of them, and then when she chose to show it. She allowed no smoking in the house, and each man had to leave his club or other weapon outside the door. Her harmonium was a great attraction, and twenty times a day she would be invited to "make the box speak"; even in the middle of baking she would have to sit down to play, her hands covered with flour! The clock, too, was an unfailing source of interest; and from one of her letters we get a vivid picture of the neat Scots girl, in her long, full skirt and demure, high-necked blouse, standing composedly in the midst of a group of naked, painted savages, who gaped with astonishment while she pointed out to them the hours at which she and her husband rose, took breakfast, tea, and dinner, when they went to bed and how long they remained there.

Agnes was filled with pity for the Tannese women. Many girl babies were left in the bush to die immediately after birth, while those who were allowed to live were sent away at an early age to their future homes to become the slaves of their husbands. The women sensed Agnes' sympathy, for, from the first, many of them came and put their arms around her, saying lovingly *"pi-nok"*—my sister. A journalist, not at all biased in favor of missionaries, who visited Tanna some years later, wrote of the shock he received when he saw "an old hag, so hideous, clad only in a grass petticoat, embrace and caress the lady with fervour. Not only a fashionable woman of the world but any working girl would shrink from such a contact with disgust. Mrs. Watt does not like it, I am sure," he continues, "but she disengages herself without any sign of repugnance. And then I understand the true missionary spirit."

A woman on Tanna was a mere nothing; but Agnes soon found that *missi bran*—the woman missionary—was more than a Tanna woman. She often wondered, she said, how sturdy warriors felt when she cleared twenty or thirty of them out of her house with a word and a smile! She found, as Captain Cook had said, that the Tannese were inveterate thieves, and she often came in from the outside bakehouse to find a number of them ransacking her drawers and cupboards, leaving smears of paint over all her belongings. She was always amazed at the way in which they managed to hide their spoil, in spite of having no clothing in which to conceal it! When she ordered them to replace what they had taken, they grumbled and looked fierce, but they always obeyed the quietly determined woman with the candid, fearless eyes. She found one man walking off with their precious American saw and ordered him to put it down. He flew into a passion and swore that he would not enter the mission premises again.

"Very well," she said quietly. "It is very good of you to come to see us, but if you do not wish to come, then that will still be good."

He looked at her in astonishment for a long time, then asked, "Do you hate me?"

"No, indeed, I love you still, as I love all my brothers."

Apparently struck to the heart by her magnanimity, he went away, but returned the next day and again demanded the saw. Agnes again refused, and as he strode to the door in anger he picked up a small hammer and said he would take that. She was between him and the door, and without flinching took the hammer out of his hand, saying he could not have it. "At this he was very angry," she related, "but I began tatting and never minded him. Very soon he was all praise, thinking that I was a very wonderful woman." She was six weeks short of her twenty-third birthday and had been about four months on Tanna when she fearlessly refused to allow this unstable savage to rob her and her husband of their irreplaceable tools.

The Tannese men were great dandies, and spent days dressing one another's hair in complicated patterns or lying in idleness on their mats while their wives—sometimes as many as four to a husband—did all the work. Agnes said roundly that the men were boasters and cowards and bullies. If a wife failed in her supposed duty to her "lord," she was rewarded with a beating or had a knife thrown at her, and Agnes could scarcely bear to hear the poor creatures screaming under the savage blows of their husbands. One of the chiefs, a regular worshiper in the little church, threw an ax at his wife, severely wounding her, for a very trivial offense. In many instances widows were strangled and buried with their husbands.

The Watts saved three poor women from this awful fate when a high chief died. They visited him a week before his death and spoke to him of Jesus as his Saviour. Agnes sat on the ground beside him, holding his hand while he looked at her with great pathos, repeating over and over, "Yesu." He promised her that his mother and his two wives should be allowed to live, and kept urging his young men to "hear the words of Missi." He asked to be buried as a Christian, without gods or muskets or *kava* (the native ceremonial drink) in the grave, and, above all, without life being taken. Not being at all sure that his people intended to carry out the chief's wishes, Agnes went with her husband to the burial and waited until they had seen the body laid in the grave, another old chief lamenting the while that "such a great man should be allowed to die without others . . . to accompany him into the next world."

"Well, Nancy," said her husband one evening, a few weeks later, "how many times have you read your mail from home since I brought it to you yesterday?"

"Just as many times as you have read yours, I expect," she retorted with a smile. "When you've been famished for letters for five whole months or more, it wouldn't seem natural to read them just once or twice, would it? I don't mind confessing now, William, that I almost dreaded to break the seal of those letters in case they contained news of illness or death or trouble among my dear ones at home. Just for a moment I almost thought that I should be happier if I hadn't a relative or friend on earth to be concerned about—except you, dearest —and happily you are always with me. But I so often tremble to think of what may be happening on the other side of the ocean, and I not to hear of it until months after."

"But I'm sure you don't feel like that for long, do you? Think, dear, if you hadn't a relative or friend in the world, you wouldn't receive those letters that bring you so much joy."

"Oh, no, William, those thoughts are only for a moment.

When I read page after page of encouragement from those who love us and are so deeply interested in what we are doing, my heart rejoices because we are not as much alone in our work as we sometimes feel we are."

"It's a great thing, Nancy, that you write them in such detail about our life and work and the people here, for very often the people at home don't seem to understand our problems very well. It's a delightful fancy to picture the new mission station being opened, and the missionary, in broadcloth, with Bible in hand, making known to wondering crowds, for the first time, the tidings of salvation. But that isn't how it happens here, is it?"

"Well, dear, you and I used to have some romantic ideas about missionary work, too, before we came out here. Remember? And I suppose we knew a good deal more about the reality even then than many of the good people at home. If only they could see the everyday life of a New Hebrides missionary, their romantic ideas would soon take flight!"

"Wouldn't they, though! Nancy, they should have seen us last week going by boat to Port Resolution; five hours' hard pulling against the wind, and you sitting up to your ankles in water most of the time. And then a picture of you surrounded by those poor women with their filthy matted hair, all of you squatting on mother earth in a native hut while you tried to muster enough words in their language to tell them about Jesus."

"Yes. Did you notice, by the way, how those women copied everything I did? If I put my hand to my face or touched my hair, they all did the same, evidently thinking it was a part of the worship. . . . I wish our friends at home could see you rethatching the roof, too, or putting on the storm rigging, or running up a new outhouse, for all the world as if you were a journeyman carpenter!"

"One thing I'm sure our friends at home fail to realize, Nancy, is how long it takes to learn a new language."

"*A* new language," she broke in. "If that were all! If only, William, all the islands in the New Hebrides had one language! If only, to be less ambitious, even each island had a common language! But look at Tanna. Already we find that the people here speak several languages, and almost every village seems to have its own dialect. I sometimes wonder whether we shall ever know enough of any one of the languages to be able not only to talk freely to the people but to translate the Bible for them."

"Well, my dear, I think you have made a very good beginning with your hymns. I suppose no one who has not undertaken the work can realize the difficulty of translating a Christian hymn into a language that has no words to describe Christian experience. With the hymns you have translated already it seems to me that you have put the central ideas of the original into very melodious Tannese verse. And how these people love to sing! Sometimes I have a vision of the gospel singing its way into their hearts when it cannot make an entry in any other way. Our two little Tannese girls appreciate your hymns anyway. I heard them singing one very sweetly before they went to bed tonight."

"I'm glad you heard them, William. Kaianga and Kauea are a great joy to me. Every time I look at them in their clean clothes, with their faces and hands well washed instead of painted, I can believe that one day all the girls and women of Tanna will be like them, modest and self-respecting, able to read and sew and sing hymns, and free from fear."

Soon their work was interrupted by a terrible outbreak of influenza, one of the scourges taken to the South Sea islands by Western "civilization." Scarcely one person known to the Watts escaped, and as soon as the dread epidemic seemed to be slackening, the people fell victims for a second and even a third time. Agnes was filled with compassion for the sick, "lying in a wretched hut, having no bed but the leaf of the coconut tree, no kind friend to minister to their wants." For the Tannese believed that no one was ever ill from natural causes; a disease maker must be burning his *nahak* (any kind of rubbish that he might have left about, such as the skin of a banana, a piece of a garment, etc.); so instead of looking after those who were sick, they merely blamed their relatives for having carelessly allowed them to fall into the power of the disease maker. The natural corollary of this idea about sickness was the belief that few, if any, Tannese died natural deaths; they must have been victims of witchcraft. And who, asks Agnes, are more likely to be blamed for sickness and death than the missionaries? Many of the people had a superstitious dread of them to begin with, believing that they had power to bring life or death. The long period of the influenza epidemic became an anxious time for the Watts. They could not watch people sicken without giving them simple remedies, such as quinine, laudanum, paregoric, and sal volatile. Yet they had to be cautious, in case the patient died and they were held responsible.

In January, 1873, Agnes had her first experience of a tropical hurricane, during which she and her husband rushed in the darkness from one outhouse and native hut to another in search of safety. In the gray light of morning a scene of utter desolation met her eyes and she confesses that she began the day with a good "greet"—cry. Every floor in the mission house was flooded with water, and the roof, thatched with sugar-cane leaf, was torn up; the church roof was damaged, the boathouse a total wreck, and fencing lay flat on the ground. What moved Agnes to tears was the attitude of the Tannese, who stood around shouting, talking, and gesticulating instead of beginning to clear up the mess. "We are homeless wanderers," her husband said to her despairingly.

As soon as the excitement subsided, however, the Tannese came forward to help, and in a surprisingly short time all the houses were made watertight, the fences repaired, and a new boathouse and cowhouse were built. As was their usual custom, the Watts paid for the work done on their own premises; but they let it be known that the church and its fence were public property and that if the people felt the worship to be a good thing, they should repair them for nothing. This invitation was responded to by thirty Tannese. Agnes, rejoicing in this evidence of their concern, boiled "a large pot of beans, another of rice, besides a piece of salt meat for their dinner."

Although unnerved by the severity of the storm and the loss of much of their small property, Agnes was troubled above everything else by fear as to the effect of the hurricane on the minds of the islanders, who believed that many people had the power to "make storm" as well as to cause sickness. Would they blame the missionaries for the disastrous hurricane, or would the shore people and the inland tribes, who were always at loggerheads, blame each other and go to war about it?

On the following Sunday the people who came to church were so excited and preoccupied that Agnes felt that she and her husband were working in vain. In spite of all they could say as to the origin of storms, the shore people were determined to lay the blame on those tribes inland with whom they were perpetually in a state of feud. In a bid to stop a war between the tribes, which would jeopardize their work, William and Agnes went off early on Monday morning to see the leaders of the inland people. They took with them the young girl, Kauea, whom they had adopted and who had come from that district. After much talking to and fro they succeeded in extracting a promise that the inland tribes would not fight. Back they hastened to their own people by the shore and gathered them all together in the public square. To their delight they found that they had already agreed not to make war on their hereditary enemies, because if they fought, their plantations of yams would go to ruin, and the hurricane had already destroyed much of their food.

The rebuilding and rethatching brought a great deal of extra work to Agnes. In a letter home she pictures her friends asking, "But what have you to do with all that building?" "Well," she replies, "I bought all the thatch, and am still buying it, although I have got upwards of five hundred roots already." Buying by barter, of course, was a serious and lengthy process, quite different from buying for cash in a market with fixed prices. "Then," she goes on, "I have to see that the workers get some food, besides helping William with my sage advice." Amid "the bustle of building, thatching, bartering, etc." they were spending two days a week printing a copy of the hymns that Agnes had translated. The Glasgow Foundry Boys' Religious Society, which helped the mission consistently through the years, had sent out some large type, but only enough to print one page at a time, so that the process was slow and laborious. Later the Society sent out more type, which was of great value not only to the Watts but to missionaries on other islands in the group.

The year 1875 on Tanna was a period of earthquakes (twenty-seven, most of considerable severity, in less than three months), hurricanes, war between rival factions, murders, suicides, and threats. The mission house was to be burned again and again, and even those who had become regular church attenders began to talk about "making an oven" for some of their enemies. After reading a detailed account of these occurrences, in which the Watts received a full share of unwelcome attention, including a volley of bullets fired at them, we feel that perhaps Agnes is understating the case when she remarks, "I must confess I felt rather uneasy," adding the significant remark, "In this state of uncertainty we slept but little." Notwithstanding war, general excitement, and hurricanes, however, the Watts succeeded in getting a new grass church and other buildings put up, Agnes acting as architect. "While the natives were running off day after day to fight, their missionary was busy correcting and printing the Parables of our Lord, and I kept up our daily sewing school." To the repeated complaint of the Aneityumese teachers that "these are times to flee, not to build," the missionaries replied firmly, "You can flee if you like; as yet we see no cause to flee."

About this time a proposal was made to transfer the Watts to Aneityum, but the synod was against their leaving Tanna. The reasons, which Agnes mentions playfully in a letter to her father, give an insight into the value of their work: "They said that were we to leave Tanna the island would go down; nobody could fill our places there; that *Mrs.* Watt (not Mr. Watt, mind you) had the true ring of a Tannese linguist;

and to take us off Tanna would be to write ichabod over it. . . . If we long for fame and the praise of the churches, this is the sphere."

Kwamera, the Watts's station, was on the weather side of Tanna, exposed to the full force of the southeast trade winds. It had no harbor and the only opening through the coral reef was so narrow that the *Dayspring* and other ships had to lie outside, sometimes for days, until the sea moderated sufficiently to allow passengers and stores to be landed in boats. Every time she left the island Agnes had to endure this nerve-racking journey between ship and shore, the ship's boat tossing alarmingly, waves breaking over and drenching the occupants to the skin. Then, while both the ship and the small boat alongside slid sickeningly into the trough of the waves and the gale howled through the rigging, she had to climb up the vessel's side, every lurch threatening to tear her clinging fingers from the ladder.

Once on board the mission ship, however, Agnes began to enjoy herself, unless the weather was very rough, when she became "very meek" and was glad to lie down. "What a gathering and all in a small vessel," she writes. "At times we have missionaries with their wives and children, white men from the captain to the sailors, black men from the king of one of our islands, or a part of it, to the most degraded of the devil's slaves. We have cows, pigs, goats and fowls!" And all packed into a tiny sailing ship of one hundred and fifty tons!

In 1882 the Neilsons had to leave the mission station at Port Resolution, and the Watts added it to their charge at Kwamera, living at each place in turn. The distance by land between the two was only some eight miles, but the way was rough and hilly; and as much household gear, books, a sewing machine, and other heavy baggage had to be carried between the stations, the missionaries more often than not made the journey in their own whale boat with Tannese boatmen. During one hot season they visited Port Resolution six times by boat and twice overland. Although the distance was short, the voyage in an open boat was often dangerous and uncomfortable, and at times they were detained for a week or more by high winds and heavy seas. Agnes writes of one trip: "We did have a spin through the water; we surged and raced along like a race yacht, taking in a spray now and again. Having a very heavy load of corrugated iron. . . . I felt sure we would sink like lead if we took a sea on board, such as we had done nine years ago when we barely escaped being swamped. I am not ashamed to say I was nervous, though I contrived not to show it. . . . I believe a year of life and hard work is not so wearing to me as an hour in the boat in such weather; and yet this year I have travelled sixty miles of open sea, round a coral-bound coast, and generally we have had rough trips."

The Watts kept a large establishment at Kwamera, sometimes as many as twenty men, women, and children being entirely dependent on them for food, shelter, and clothing. As supplies only arrived on the island twice a year and might be delayed by shipwreck or a hurricane, the missionaries had to provide most of their own comforts, and their helpers tended goats, poultry, and the garden. Housekeeping was no light task in the sweltering heat, with no labor-saving appliances, and a larger staff was necessary than in civilization. But the main reason for involving themselves in the expense and trouble of so many helpers was that "Tanna is a hard field, and except by taking them into our establishment, we have found it difficult to get any one to wait on regular instruction." Their own people came to worship every evening, with a few outsiders, and most of them remained for lessons in reading and writing. Their textbooks at first were Agnes' translations of English hymns, then St. Matthew's Gospel, and gradually other books of the New Testament as the Watts translated them.

Agnes held sewing classes regularly for the women, who helped her to make hundreds of women's dresses, patchwork quilts, and men's and boys' sweaters. Some people at home, she felt, thought that the missionaries put too much importance on clothing, but among the natives it was the badge of Christianity. When a new tribe "took the worship," as they expressed it, then the cry was for clothing. If a man became disaffected toward the church, one of his first acts was to lay aside the cloth or girdle that he had begun to wear. Agnes generally had blisters on her fingers from cutting out so many garments, and as material often ran short, her inventive powers were severely taxed. On one occasion she was driven to tear up every sheet she could possibly spare, and she even made dresses out of a sofa cover. She taught the women to sew together the remnants from the dresses to make bright handkerchiefs for their heads.

March, 1879, was a landmark in Agnes' life, for in that month she and her husband reached Scotland on their first furlough, and she was able to spend eleven months with the dearly loved members of her large family. In May of the following year they landed again in Tanna, to be met by gaunt and hungry people. Another terrible hurricane had swept the island, leaving uprooted trees and shattered houses in its wake. The sea had washed up inside the mission house fence, and the house itself looked very dreary to Agnes "after the nice well-carpeted rooms I had lately left." Many of the people had died or been killed in their absence, and those who remained were almost starving through the loss of their food crops, eking out a bare existence on roots and leaves. The Watts distributed all the flour and rice they had, but Agnes was saddened by "the bairns coming round with hungry faces, and having nothing to give them." At the end of a month the *Dayspring* called again, and they sailed in her round the other islands in the group, buying from the missionaries flour, rice, and beans to take back to their starving flock on Tanna.

After her visit home, Agnes seemed to feel even more the separation from her family. In June, 1881, she writes that for many months she has been buried alive or banished, without the remotest chance of sending off or receiving mail. "Often have I said," she sighs, "that the four hurricane months looked like a tunnel to me. I fear to enter, and I breathe freely when I reach the farther end. The longer I am here, I feel it more. Perhaps never since our settlement have we been so shut up as during the past year."

Later that same year, however, the church was established on Tanna, more than forty years after the first Christian teachers landed, and twelve years after the Watts first settled at Kwamera. William baptized two men, four women, and three children, and the following Sunday, he and Agnes had the solemn joy of uniting with their first Tannese converts in the Sacrament of the Lord's Supper. Agnes was deeply hurt by the prevalent opinion that no good thing was ever likely to come out of this island that had resisted the gospel for so long. "Tanna *is* a hard field," she agrees, "but is *that* any reason why we should give the people up? Or send men past Tanna, saying, 'Wherever you go, don't go to Tanna; Tanna is doomed!'? We trust in God that poor doomed Tanna shall yet shake herself from the dust. . . . To us who labor down in this deep mine of heathenism, in darkness, loneliness and longing, receiving, from time to time, from those who are working in the light and sunshine of social life, messages to the effect that we are wasting our time, spending our strength in vain, and digging where gold can never be found —it is cheering to realize that to our Master we stand or fall. Besides we never know when, in digging, we may strike the precious ore."

But soon Agnes herself was having to bewail "dark, dark Tanna. She sells the bodies and souls of her children for a piece of pork and a drink of *kava*." A twelve-year-old girl, brought up as a Christian in the Watts's household, was dragged away in a canoe, "as if she had been a pig," to be taken to a heathen district to be married. Agnes felt Wabu's fate so keenly that she neither ate nor slept for three days, the poor girl's cries as she was being carried off ringing constantly in her ears. So many times she had known the grief of having one whom she had watched over, taught, nursed, and prayed for compelled to return to her former heathen life.

The church was formed, but it did not grow. Two of the first members died, the youngest and most promising, and the church was blamed. A regular attendant at the services died also, and people advised one another to shun the gospel for fear that they, too, might not have long to live. The congregation of a hundred shrank because of this superstitious fear; but the hardest blow of all was the backsliding of one of the only two men who were full church members. The people were not ignorant of the gospel; indeed, Agnes writes that they had a vast amount of Scripture knowledge, that they even said that "the message is good." But they always added, "How can we give up the customs of our fathers?" The missionaries felt they could do no more; only an outpouring of the Holy Spirit could quicken the dormant seed. "Pray, pray for us," Agnes begged, "not in a general way, but that this very year the dawn may come." But whether the dawn came that year or not, she was confident in her faith that "sooner or later Tanna will be won for Christ," although, she added wistfully, "it requires more faith to preach to dry bones than to living men."

During the years 1881-1889 the Watts were in charge also of the island of Aniwa. The additional work was a terrible tax on their strength, as each of their frequent visits entailed wearisome tossings in the stuffy cabin of the *Dayspring*, companioned by cockroaches, sometimes for a week on end if the winds were contrary or heavy seas made landing impossible. They generally remained for six weeks or two months at a time, and had to transport almost all the stores and household equipment they would need, even including goats and fowls, with Tannese to look after them. But the people of Aniwa were so different in character from the Tannese, so peaceable and eager for the gospel, that Agnes often referred to the island as her Bethany, where they were received with loving gratitude and encouraged by the growth of a fine Christian church, which actually sent teachers to help with the evangelization of Tanna.

The great ingathering that the Watts yearned and prayed for did not come, but a few breaks in the clouds made their hearts rejoice. "I live for Tanna (indeed many think I have

Tanna on the brain) and will die for it, if need be," Agnes writes passionately. With unshaken loyalty she defends the Tannese; for all their waywardness and stubbornness they are an affectionate people, she declares, and is it any wonder that she loves them? The return to Sunday worship of two men who had not entered the church for six years brought a glow to her heart; and they were "strong on hymns in terrible Tanna," singing them with a loud voice, "if not very skilfully."

William spent about ten weeks in 1889 printing and binding a catechism in Tannese and a new edition of the Tannese hymnal, which had grown to eighty-two hymns, most of them translated by Agnes. It was a laborious task by hand, and several times Agnes was alarmed because William showed symptoms of lead poisoning.

Toward the end of that year they returned once more to their native Scotland, carrying with them the fruit of years of quiet plodding—their translation of the whole of the New Testament into Tannese, which was published by the National Bible Society of Scotland. For months most of their waking moments were taken up with revising and correcting proofs, and when the New Testament was finished, Agnes compiled and translated an illustrated epitome of the Old Testament. By this time she had lost her fear of speaking in public, and her matronly figure and mellow voice became familiar to audiences in many parts of the country. Her beautiful singing of Tannese hymns, and graphic descriptions of the island people and their need, deepened and strengthened the consecration of the home church to the cause to which she was devoting her life. Returning to Tanna via Canada, the Watts were particularly happy to spend time in the church in Nova Scotia that had sent out John Geddie to the New Hebrides.

When they reached Tanna again early in 1891 they found that four out of their small band of eight church members had died, to the great distress of the others, who were convinced that there must be some fatality connected with church membership. The distribution of the New Testaments in their own language was a great event to the Tannese who were attached to the church, and gave a needed impetus to the reading classes. Inter-tribal war had broken out more fiercely than the Watts could remember it; the number of deaths was unusually large and the atrocities particularly horrible. Agnes was almost heartbroken by the callousness of a man who regularly attended church service. Coming across the mutilated body of a woman killed in the fighting and left to be devoured by dogs, he made no attempt to bury it, but remarked nostalgically, "If only the gospel had not reached my village, how I would have enjoyed a feast off you!"

Eighteen ninety-two was to Agnes the most trying year she had spent on Tanna. Another terrible epidemic of influenza scourged them, and in nine months three of the most promising young women in the church died. The heathen Tannese exulted, "We are right. The gospel kills, for are not all the Christian girls dying?" In three years no new members had joined the church, and the small membership had been more than halved by death. Agnes was grieved by murmurs that the backwardness of the gospel on Tanna was due to want of faith on the part of the missionaries, and was grateful to a warm defender who contended that only those who had "*gigantic* faith" could have labored for so many years in that unproductive field.

For a year or two before their second furlough the Watts had begun to travel far and wide among the villages, and they resumed these visits on their return. They often spent several nights away from home, spreading a cotton mat for a bed in a grass hut and covering themselves with mosquito netting to keep off lizards and rats as well as insects. Toiling up mountain paths in blazing sunshine or splashing through mud-choked valleys in tropical rain, clambering over rocks or through sinking sand on the seashore, holding services several times a day whenever they could get a group of Tannese together, and dealing with as many sick people as if they were qualified "medicals" was exhausting work for the two middle-aged pioneers, especially as Agnes developed a tumor on one foot that made walking particularly painful. But though jaded in body, they were encouraged by the welcome given them in many of the places and by "the blessedness of sowing the seed of the gospel." Agnes had a heart open to beauty, and was uplifted by the mountain ranges towering four thousand feet into the blue sky, and soothed by the drowsy loveliness of the valleys where magnificent tree ferns waved their graceful fronds in every passing breeze. When she arrived hot and tired at the top of a steep rise with lungs almost bursting, she felt rewarded by the wide view over the ocean toward the distant islands, and by the benediction of the cooling sea breezes.

In 1893 Agnes was able to record some encouragement: three new church members, three Christian marriages, one new station opened and an old one renewed. The Christians, too, had begun to realize the joy of giving, and brought eleven bags of copra, the proceeds of the sale being sent to the Presbyterian Church of New Zealand. Perhaps an even more hopeful sign was that six Tannese men in different places had become definite helpers in the church, calling their fellow villagers to regular prayer. They had not gone very far in the Christian way, but they were very much in earnest, and Agnes told her friends what a decided advance it was for men on Tanna to be ready to take any position of Christian leadership at all.

A few months later, in April, 1894, Agnes was taken suddenly ill. Within an hour she was dead, at the early age of forty-eight, and was buried at the very spot on which she had first set foot on Tanna exactly twenty-five years earlier. She impressed all who knew her, not by brilliant gifts or accomplishments, but by the beauty of her Christlike character and the power of her unquenchable faith. Like a piece of homespun tweed from her native land, her qualities were of the right kind for dependable wear. In the words of a letter to her husband from the directors of the National Bible Society of Scotland, "It could have been no ordinary woman who, after long service in a remote corner, evokes the grateful recognition of her worth from a Board meeting at the opposite end of the earth."

Lillias Underwood

When Lillias Horton was married to Horace Grant Underwood in March, 1889, they set out on a strange and adventurous wedding trip. They had met as fellow missionaries in Korea, and were married in its capital, Seoul. The Korean queen sent her gift of one million "cash" to the bride on the backs of many pack ponies, the jingling bells on their harness making early morning music in the courtyard. Translated into American currency, at that time the value of this cumbersome Arabian Nights gift was about three hundred and seventy-five dollars.

"It seemed to me," wrote Lillias, "that no honeymoon so rich in delight could ever have been planned before, and I looked forward with the greatest pleasure to a journey through a lovely country, to be filled with blessed service." Yet the missionaries and other foreigners residing in Seoul resorted to everything but force to prevent her going. They predicted that if she returned at all it would be in her coffin, and Horace Underwood fell under heavy public censure for consenting to take her into the interior of Korea, where no white woman had ever been, for until five years earlier Westerners had not been admitted into Korea at all. The white men who had ventured outside the shelter of the city walls, except to reach the port, could be counted on the fingers of one hand. Horace Underwood was one of them, however, and as he had made two journeys without succumbing to the ferocity of tigers, leopards, or Korean bandits, to bad water or contagious diseases, or the fatigue of long, forced marches, his bride felt that she could well trust his judgment. In spite of decrees forbidding foreigners to go into the interior, government officials in Seoul had given Underwood a very generous passport directing local officials to supply anything that he might require, the bills to be paid when he returned to the city.

Her husband devised a carrying chair for Lillias in which she felt "far too much babyfied for a hardy missionary." Under a bamboo roof covered with oiled and painted paper, she sat Turkish fashion on cushions with a hot-water bottle and foot-muff at her feet, and a shawl draped round the inside of the blue muslin "walls" to keep out the draughts. When the front curtain was buttoned down she was out of the range of curious eyes. Four coolies alternated in carrying the chair in pairs, three miles at a time, so that the travelers were able to make thirty or more miles a day. Lillias became used to being carried along a tolerable road, the chair swaying to a regular rhythm interrupted by an upward jolt of several inches. But she did not relish the many occasions on which the bearers—perhaps in the half-light of dawn or late in the evening—picked their way over narrow, slippery paths between half-submerged rice fields or across intervening ditches.

During the weary hours when Lillias was jolted along in the chair, her husband riding his horse behind, and their line of pack ponies and retainers stretching into the distance, she had leisure to think back over the past year into which so many new and vivid impressions had been crowded.

She had arrived from the United States the previous spring with a degree in medicine and nursing experience in a Chicago hospital, and had joined the small Presbyterian family in Korea. "How hopeless looked the task we had before us in those days," she wrote later. "A little company of scarce a dozen people, including our Methodist brethren, many of us able to stammer only a few words of the language as yet, attempting to introduce Christianity into a nation of fourteen or more millions of people, in the place of their long-established religions; and beginning with a few poor farmers and old women. But the elements of success, the certainty of victory, lay in the divine nature of the religion, and in the Almighty God who sent us with it. This knowledge inspired us and this alone."

Although the religions of Korea were long established, Lillias discovered that actually the majority of the people had lost faith in any religion. With many of them only respect for ancient customs and public opinion kept them even to the outward forms of worship. Women, and the more ignorant among the men, feared an infinite number of evil deities— gods or demons—who had to be propitiated with prayers and sacrifices, drum-beating and the ringing of bells, and many other ceremonial acts. The worship of ancestors was the religious rite that had the strongest hold upon the people, and as this was, of course, forbidden to Christians, those who embraced the new faith risked being looked upon as traitors to the most sacred obligations of family and home. Yet unassuaged spiritual hunger led many Koreans to receive the gospel gladly, to take Christ's yoke upon them and find in him the joy and power that their ancient religions could not give them.

The most illustrious of Lillias' patients was the Korean queen, to whom she was officially appointed medical attendant. She responded to her first summons to the palace with some trepidation. The missionaries' foothold in the country was precarious and she feared that through ignorance of Korean customs she might give offense, so that their developing work would be hindered or stopped. She had been warned never to visit the palace except in full court dress, but discovered to her consternation that the two gowns that she had brought for the purpose had both been ruined during their long journey across the Pacific. As she looked at her plain "best" dress, she ruefully decided that it certainly did not look like court attire and hoped that she would not be considered lacking in respect. She did not realize how well it became her slight, graceful figure, nor how likely it was that her eager smile would easily win forgiveness for a few breaches of etiquette.

The king and queen graciously rose to receive her when she entered the audience chamber. She smiled when she recalled the unexpected emotions with which she, a descendant of revolutionary Americans, bowed low on entering the royal presence.

The queen, like most Korean women, was not beautiful according to Western standards, but vivacity and wit combined with high intelligence to give her face character and charm. Through an interpreter, who stood behind a tall screen, she asked the visitor many questions about her family and friends, her upbringing, the voyage to Korea, and about American life and customs.

After these polite preliminaries Lillias inquired about her royal patient's health. Her difficulties in communicating on this subject through an interpreter were nothing to those of the Korean doctors, always men, who had attended her majesty before the coming of the missionaries. Korean etiquette would not allow of their being in the same room as the queen, so they "felt" her pulse by means of a long cord fastened round her wrist and carried into the next room, and looked at her tongue when she protruded it through a slit in a screen. Lillias found that the queen had a small tumor or boil and innocently proposed to lance it. The mere suggestion of approaching the sacred person with a surgical instrument, however, caused a storm of indignation and horror from the queen's attendants, and the slight operation was absolutely forbidden by the king. Lillias prescribed a course of treatment that would eventually disperse the growth, and then she and the missionary's wife who had accompanied her bowed themselves backwards out of the royal apartments "as if we had been born and bred hangers-on of courts."

At this point in her reverie her husband drew alongside on his horse and they exchanged a smile of perfect understanding. "Well, my dear," he said, "we are getting near the village where we shall have our midday meal, so prepare to be mobbed by the sightseers. I had better shut you up in your chair now or by Korean standards you will not be considered respectable."

Laughing gaily as he buttoned down the front flap of the chair, she called back, "I don't suppose a lion or an elephant ever created such excitement in an American village as does this one poor foreign woman in Korea. I feel just as if I were a wild animal in a show."

A small crowd was already besieging the inn, for the word had mysteriously gone round that the foreigners were to stop there. The coolies carried the closed chair into the women's room and Lillias heaved a sigh of relief as she stepped out. Furtive noises drew her attention to the paper-covered doors and windows. To her dismay they were punctured with holes made by dampening the finger and pressing it gently against the paper, and at each hole was a hungry eye watching her every movement. Her husband came in and together they hung shawls and raincoats around the room in front of the doors and windows. They sat down to their lunch, a trunk serving as table. A smothered laugh caused them to turn round. The crowd outside, not to be balked, had thrust long, slender rods through the peep-holes and lifted the improvised curtains, while multitudes of curious eyes were applied to new holes.

Lillias looked at her husband with comical despair. "If only we were ordinary travelers," she murmured, "and not missionaries! Then a syringe filled with water and well aimed at the peep-holes would give those prying people the surprise of their lives!" With pretended disapproval he shook his head at the piquant face alight with mischief. "As it is," she went on more soberly, "I try to remember that these are the people whom we are longing to serve and win. I keep on praying for patience to bear all these small annoyances cheerfully, just as you do, for the sake of bringing them to Christ."

"Yes," he replied gently, "we must remember how our Master welcomed the crowds that thronged about him. It isn't easy, but you and I are trying to follow in his footsteps by healing these people and preaching to them the words of life."

Another crowd gathered round the inn where they spent that night. Lillias was full of admiration for the patience and good humor of her husband in handling the jostling throng. He deftly isolated those who wanted medical advice and dispensed the medicines that Lillias prescribed. He rounded up some of the less boisterous of the onlookers and talked to them briefly and simply about the gospel, pressing tracts into their hands before leaving them to talk to another group.

After supper the young couple, so recently married, thought how romantic the moonlight looked and decided that they would like a walk. To go out through the gate would be to invite as escort the entire able-bodied population of the village; but the wall was low, and waiting until all seemed quiet, they crept stealthily like a couple of criminals out of their stuffy room and were over the wall, "for once alone, away from staring eyes, to enjoy the sweet air and each other's company." But a dog immediately set up a loud and continuous barking. One doorway after another was filled with white-clad forms and a swelling stream of people hastened after them up the hillside. Sadly they retraced their steps, attended by a long retinue, and hastily hid themselves once more in the dingy guest room. They looked at the dirty mats covering the earth floor on which they were supposed to sleep. Lillias shuddered as she wondered how many people had died of smallpox, cholera, typhus, or dysentery on those identical mats. They sent out for some bundles of fresh, clean straw used for thatching roofs and spread them at least a foot high. On these they made their bed, safe from the ravages of vermin, which "ploughed their weary way uselessly through the mazes of that straw all night."

"Whatever are all those soldiers doing, Horace?" Lillias asked breathlessly one morning a week or two later. "Do you think they've come to arrest us?"

"Hardly," he replied smiling. "Not with all those trumpets and drums and flags. I think they've been sent out to welcome us to Kangai. The city is only three miles away, you know."

Louder and louder grew the din as more bands and more soldiers joined in. The triumphal procession swept into the city, trumpets braying and flags flying. Boys, dancing girls, and hooligans of all descriptions laughed, jostled, and shouted around the covered chair in which Lillias, who could hear but not see them, experienced the sensations of a mouse in the power of a playful tiger.

"Looking back on it all now," she wrote long afterwards, "in the light of all that has since occurred, it was in a way fitting that the first heralds of the Gospel and the advent of Christianity in this province should be with banners, trumpets and great acclaim. The Kingdom had come, if only in its smallest beginnings, and had come to stay."

The next day an ingenious way of getting a glimpse of the foreign woman presented itself. Everyone suddenly felt the need of a doctor, and they stood in long rows from morning till night while she prescribed for real and imaginary ailments. "I might have charged almost any price," she wrote. "But I was only too glad to be able to tell them of the great Physician, whose unspeakable gift is without money or price."

After Kangai, their way lay through wildly beautiful and

sparsely populated mountain country where bands of robbers and escaped criminals lived in hiding. The magistrate at Kangai, who was a relative of the queen, had provided them with an escort consisting of a police officer and a soldier to insure their safety. One day the Underwoods hurried ahead with the soldier to their midday resting place at a tiny inn. Their grooms and other attendants arrived later, surrounded by about twenty or thirty wild-looking men, with fierce, blood-shot eyes. These men had accused one of the grooms of theft, had bound him, and taken possession of the missionaries' loads. Peering through a crack in the door, Lillias saw her husband in the midst of this wild throng, the robbers shouting angrily and brandishing their short, stout clubs.

Some of the ruffians crept up behind and pinioned the arms of Underwood and the soldier as they stood shoulder to shoulder in a narrow passage holding off their assailants in front. One by one they carried off the grooms and other servants, and, finally, the policeman. Only the Underwoods and the soldier were left. Lillias felt her heart turn to ice when the robbers returned once more to carry off her husband, openly threatening to murder him, saying it was the only way in which to treat foreigners. At this, however, the villagers intervened. The Underwoods, they said, were known at the palace and carried passports; the village would be punished if they were killed. As the villagers could identify the criminals, they held them in their power, and the robbers sullenly took themselves off.

The nearest magistrate was twenty-five miles away. For their own safety, and also to secure the release of their captive servants and the return of their goods, the Underwoods decided that they had better try to reach him that night. Lillias, as she confessed afterwards, was "a very much frightened woman, and my whole desire was to run away as fast and as far as possible from that dreadful locality." Just as they were leaving, two or three country folk arrived and asked for medicines for trifling complaints. Impatiently Lillias turned to her husband. "Oh, do send them away, Horace. We can't possibly wait to do anything for them. We must just get away as quickly as ever we can."

"But these men and women need help, Lillias, and we can give it to them. Don't you think we must show them that the servants of Jesus are never in too much of a hurry to be kind? It won't take long—and anyway, dear, aren't we in God's hands?"

So Lillias prescribed for afflicted eyes and ears and throats, her own eyes and ears fearing every moment to see and hear the ruffians returning to carry away her husband and herself to torture or death. She hoped afterwards that, distraught as she was, she had not poisoned any of her patients! The last sufferer was seen and the medicines were repacked. Then another patient appeared, and another and another. Out came the medicine chest again. Lillias prescribed, her husband prepared the medicines. At last they were free to leave.

Their way led up the mountainside among great boulders. Fearfully, Lillias looked around, expecting at any moment to see their enemies spring from ambush. When she turned to her husband and said, "Well, there's nothing left to do but trust the Lord," it flashed over them both how often Christians only trust him when there is nothing else to do, as if his help were a last forlorn hope. To their joy they found that the Korean magistrate, whose house they reached late that night, was an old friend from Seoul. He immediately sent out a large party of hunters who finally released the captured grooms and arrested the criminals.

Before leaving the town of the hospitable magistrate, the Underwoods gave a dinner for him and his friends. With much ingenuity they prepared a six-course meal over a bowl of charcoal and with practically no kitchen utensils, serving soup, fish, "a bewitching little roast pig" (to use Lillias' droll description) well decorated with wreaths and berries, accompanied by apple sauce, and stuffed with potatoes, chestnuts and onions, biscuits spread with marmalade for dessert, and coffee sweetened with honey. "Trifling as it may look," Lillias wrote, "for missionaries to be planning menus and giving dinners to country magistrates, there are more ways of furthering the Cause than preaching only. The hearts of the people must be won, and he who wins most friends wins the readiest and most attentive audience, one inclined in advance to favor and accept what he has to teach, and nothing is trifling which helps."

They reached Weju on the south side of the border between Korea and Manchuria. Korean Christian workers had been stationed there for some months and over a hundred applicants presented themselves for baptism. Some of them had no inkling of the real meaning of Christianity and were merely anxious to be in touch with rich and influential foreigners, who would find them speedy employment in the mission.

After much anxious examination and earnest prayer, the missionaries selected thirty-three men, not those who answered most glibly or appeared the best informed but those who gave well-nigh unmistakable evidence of sincerity of heart and true knowledge of Jesus Christ. The representative of the United States government had forbidden the baptism of converts in Korea for fear of the consequences. Foreigners were not supposed to travel through the country but to confine themselves to certain cities, so they crossed the river into Manchuria for the solemn service. The thirty-three men were the only converts baptized during the trip and they brought the total number of Protestant converts in Korea to something over a hundred since the first Korean had been baptized secretly three years earlier, in July, 1886.

Twenty-five years later Lillias heard from a missionary in that part of Korea of the phenomenal growth of one of the seeds of the gospel—small as a grain of mustard seed—that they had planted there. An elderly Korean woman from a distant city visited Weju soon after the Underwoods left. She met a friend who had seen them and heard from her what she could remember of their teaching. The woman took back to her own city three rules of faith and practice: "There is only one God and we must worship no other." "We must put away our sins, be good and pure and true." "We must keep one day in seven holy and sing the words, *Nothing but the blood of Jesus.*" Her best friend soon believed with her, and the changed lives of the two women attracted much attention in the community. Two of the leading men of the city joined them, one of whom had been notorious for his evil life. One by one, others believed because of the evidence of changed lives, and when at length a Korean colporteur came their way, he found a group of believers worshiping and serving God as best they knew. He left them with hymn books and catechisms and the knowledge of a Saviour who had died for them. By the time Lillias heard that story the small seed that she and her husband had sown, quickened by God's mighty power, had grown into a church of seven hundred members.

Their return journey to Seoul by the main road was uneventful. Horace surrounded his bride in the carrying chair with masses of lilies of the valley, lilacs, eglantine, and sweet-scented violets. They reached home about the middle of May, their unique honeymoon having lasted for more than two months. They had traveled over a thousand miles, treated over six hundred patients, and talked with many times that number.

After the birth of her son, Horace H. Underwood, in the autumn of 1890, Lillias was very ill, but the doctors agreed that her life might possibly be saved by a visit to America. She felt bitterly ashamed at being the cause of her husband's leaving Korea for a time, when workers were pitiably few and the need was so great. But he pleaded the cause of Korea so ably in the West that several new missionaries volunteered, and American, Canadian, and British Christians were roused to greater interest in spreading the gospel among its people.

On her return to Korea, Lillias carried on again her interrupted medical work, and as her knowledge of the language increased to the point where she could talk and pray with freedom, she started women's meetings. With money collected in America she bought and enlarged a house on a breezy hillside, named the Shelter, as a hospital for patients with infectious diseases, who would otherwise have been thrust into the streets by the Koreans and left to die. At the same time she opened a little dispensary, where, in addition to medical work, she held women's Bible classes.

Lillias became a familiar figure at the court, and after she was able to dispense with the formality of an interpreter when talking with the queen, she often forgot that she was not chatting with an intimate friend. This friendship laid an even heavier burden of responsibility on her, and she begged the other missionaries to pray that an opportunity might be given to her to speak to the queen about Christ, and that she might make the best use of it. On Christmas Eve the queen sent for her and asked her all about the great Christian festival, its origin and meaning and how it was celebrated. Here was the opportunity for which Lillias had longed and prayed. She told the queen the gospel story, of the Babe in the manger who was the Son of God, sent to save his people from their sins.

The queen begged Lillias to bring her little son to the palace as often as possible, and on each occasion he was petted and fed until his mother feared for his manners and his digestion. All Koreans, she found, were extremely fond of children, who were an open sesame to their hearts and homes at all times. "God blesses the missionary babies," she wrote. "These little preachers open doors that yield to no other touch than their little dimpled fingers."

In 1895 a terrible epidemic of Asiatic cholera swept the land. The Shelter was filled with patients under the supervision of Dr. Wells and the Underwoods. No nurses were to be had and Christian converts were asked to help them for the love of Christ. Some of these men were of the scholar and gentleman class who had never done manual work of any kind. After the first natural hesitation, they responded with Christian loving-kindness and became faithful and devoted nurses, never shirking the most repellent task. Cholera is a loathsome disease, and only love made it possible for them to nurse its victims without sensations of overwhelming disgust.

Every evening a service of prayer and praise was held in the central court of the Shelter, where the doctors and nurses renewed their faith and love. Of the one hundred and seventy-three patients whom they treated, one hundred and twelve, or a percentage of sixty-five, recovered, while elsewhere about sixty-five per cent died. Lillias attributed this result in part to the conscientious and untiring nursing by the Korean Christians. Koreans who saw the missionaries watching over the sick night and day were heard to say to one another, "How these foreigners love us! Would we do as much for our own kin as they do for strangers?"

As a result of the Chino-Japanese war, which was fought in Korea during 1894, the Japanese proclaimed the independence of that country, but in practice established a protectorate and directed Korean policy at home and abroad. Many public offices were filled by Japanese citizens or pro-Japanese Koreans, and a large body of Korean troops was under the command of Japanese officers. Lillias Underwood's friend, the patriotic and brilliant queen, was an obstacle to these Japanese plans, and on the eighth of October, 1895, Japanese cutthroats, under the eyes of Japanese army officers, rushed the palace guard and murdered her. The king, distraught by the loss of his idolized queen, signed documents by which he handed authority over to the usurping government. As he went in fear of being poisoned, Lillias and the ladies from one of the European legations alternated in sending him specially prepared dishes in a tin box provided with a Yale lock. Underwood was acting as interpreter to the United States minister, who, with the representatives of other foreign powers, tried to protect the royal family from further outrage. He carried messages between the legations and the palace several times a day and was able to place the key of the box in the king's own hands. For weeks after the assassination of the queen the missionaries took it in turns, two by two, to stand on guard at the palace, as it was felt that the traitors would hesitate to harm the king in the presence of foreign witnesses. Lillias Underwood and the other wives, however, as they waited anxiously for their husbands' return, were in little doubt that, if the rebels considered it necessary to dispose of the king, they would not hesitate to kill the witnesses, also.

Four months later the king escaped to the Russian legation, the Japanese-controlled government was overthrown, and Japanese influence in Korean affairs was stemmed for a time.

Lillias made several more journeys into the interior with her husband and son (who was first initiated into missionary travel at the age of six). Everywhere they found that some of the seed sown on previous journeys had sprung up and borne fruit "some sixty and some an hundredfold." Their small boy was an ambassador of good will, and in one of her letters the mother gives a charming picture of her mingled pride and apprehension when she watched him walking in the center of a row of seven or eight Korean boys of his own age, the dirtiest in the town, with his arm around one on either side, all chatting and laughing together. The care of a child on these journeys was no light matter, for he had not the same immunity from the many diseases of the country that his parents had acquired. Lillias was horrified on one occasion to learn that a child ill with smallpox had been taken out of a village home that the three Underwoods might have her room. Without knowing this, they had eaten and slept in that infected room, and had even used the family's cooking utensils, spoons, and bowls, before their packs had arrived.

Both mother and doctor in Lillias reacted instantaneously. She sent a swift messenger with a dispatch to the nearest telegraph station twenty-four hours away. In response a speedy runner arrived a week later with virus from the missionary doctor in Pyeng Yang to whom she had appealed.

Everywhere on these later journeys they received touching evidence of the simple faith with which so many Koreans had received the gospel message, often at second or third hand. "Where is Jesus?" Lillias asked one old woman. "He's right here with me all the time," she answered promptly. "Yes, but where else is he?" Confused and troubled that she could not satisfy the white teacher, she said, "I'm only a poor ignorant old woman and I don't know where else he is, but I *know* he is right here in my house all the time."

Wherever they went Lillias treated patients in the morning; in the afternoon she held Bible classes for the women and taught the children to sing hymns. Many of the older women were ill favored and coarsened by hard work, but she always seemed to love them at first sight, so strong was the bond between her and them in Christ. They were "so hungry for truth, so eager to learn, so full of humble loving interest in every word, with such a spirit of child-like faith." These Korean women led a hard life, standing to serve their husbands while they ate, working while their menfolk smoked at leisure. Lillias was glad to notice that in many of the Christian homes the woman's load was lightened as the man began to follow the example of her own husband's loving care for her. All along the road, where only a few years before they had found absolute ignorance of the gospel, they found evidences of the dawning light. Everywhere people had heard of the "Jesus doctrine," and heard well of it. One man had been in the cholera hospital in Seoul and had seen Lillias weeping over a poor coolie whom all her efforts had failed to keep alive. He searched until he found the God who filled his worshipers with such love, and when he had found him he preached him to others. The Underwoods visited two villages that he had influenced. In each of them all the people had gathered in the meeting house and he had read to them from the Gospels and tracts and taught them the catechism and hymns.

They visited an island where they found a small company of believers waiting for examination and baptism, none of whom had ever met a Western missionary. About ten o'clock on the night before they were due to leave, two women came and asked whether Lillias would go to their home to teach them a little more. She sat down with them in a poor room lit by a tiny wick burning in a saucer of oil. The hard, careworn faces of the women were transformed by the light of a glorious hope. A cough outside the door betrayed the fact that a number of men were gathered there in the cold November night, listening to such scraps of the teaching as they could hear. In deference to Korean custom, Lillias usually taught only women and kept as much out of sight as possible. But on this occasion she had to agree that the men should come in. It was a picture, she said afterwards, that she would never forget, "the dark eager faces, every one leaning forward in eager attitude, all seeking more knowledge of divine truth, hungering and thirsting after righteousness." Next morning at the first streak of dawn the women came to her again with tears streaming down their faces. "Come to us again soon," they begged; "we are so ignorant and so weak, how can we escape the snares of Satan, with no one here to lead and teach us!"

In April, 1916, after twenty-eight years spent in Korea, Lillias Underwood said farewell to her adopted country and returned to America with her husband, both of them in very feeble health. He died later that year; she published a life of him in 1918. Writing of the many dangers that they faced together, when death at times seemed very near, she quotes Kipling's line, *A reckless seraphim hanging on the rein of a red-maned star,* with the comment, "It has occurred to me that my experiences have been nearly as strenuous as that angel's, and my husband was much like that red-maned star." Words to be found in her earlier book about missionary life in Korea are an epitome of her own life: "If in these pages you have seen much that leads you to think the land is a difficult one in which to live, if you have read of political unrest, bad government, riots, robbers and plagues; if you have learned that missionaries have died of typhus fever, smallpox, dysentery and other violent forms of disease, this will only serve to remind you that the more valuable the prize to be won, the greater the difficulty and cost. If you desire to share in the joy of this great harvest, and are worthy, you will fear no danger, shrink from no obstacles, either for yourselves or for your loved ones, whom you are asked to give to the work. . . . There is no more place on the mission field for the fearful and unbelieving than in heaven itself. Let the applicants [for missionary work] be reduced until only the resolute, the consecrated, those who believe in God, the people and themselves, are accepted for this mighty privilege, this high calling."

Japanese imperial power, which received a temporary check at the end of the last century, became paramount in Korea in

1905. In the years before the outbreak of war between Japan and the Western world in 1941, increasingly strong measures were taken by Japan to bring Koreans into full subjection to their hereditary enemy. The Christian church was under constant fire. Koreans who had received the gospel at the hands of Lillias and Horace Underwood were oppressed, discriminated against, and tortured because as Christians they refused to worship the Japanese emperor as divine. Many of them became martyrs for the sake of Christ. Others gave way under the pressure of persecution. In order to isolate Korean Christians from the fellowship of the universal church, they were refused permission by the Japanese government to attend the world meeting of the International Missionary Council in India in 1938.

By the time the despotic hand of Japan was removed in 1945, the sorely tried church in Korea, although still alive, had lost most of its leaders. In the North the church was harassed by the Soviet occupying power; in the South the church courageously opened a great evangelistic campaign. But new and bitter trials awaited the people of Korea when war devastated their land in the years following 1950. The church played a notable part in reconstruction, but for years to come it will need the comradeship and help of many Christian leaders from the West with the skill, the courage, and the loving devotion of a Lillias Underwood.

THE AUTHOR

WINIFRED MATHEWS was born and educated in London. For many years she served as an editor of the United Council for Missionary Education, whose books are published under the imprint of the Edinburgh House Press. Here she not only worked with authors in preparing missionary education material, but produced several books of her own. After her marriage she worked in close collaboration with her husband, the late Basil Mathews, the well known author of many Friendship Press books. Mrs. Mathews is also the author of *The Glorious Company, Soldiers' Heroine,* and *In Convict Cells,* and for several years edited *The Colonial Review,* produced by the Colonial Department of the University of London Institute of Education. She is now living in Oxford, England.

THE ARTIST

RAFAEL PALACIOS, a former resident of Puerto Rico, is one of New York's busiest and most prolific artists. His successes in New York include a one-man show of gouaches and participation in two exhibits: the First National Art Exhibition (representing Puerto Rico) and the First Newspaper Artists' Show. He has also exhibited at the Atheneum and the University of Puerto Rico. Mr. Palacios has become known as one of the foremost cartographers in the country, and his maps may be found in *Life* Magazine and in many current books. He has illustrated three other books for Friendship Press: *The Traded Twins, He Wears Orchids,* and *Great Is the Company;* and he designed the jacket for *Under Three Flags.*